ISBN 0-8373-2144-1

C-2144   CAREER EXAMINATION SE

This is your
PASSBOOK® for...

Administrative Analyst

Test Preparation Study Guide

Questions & Answers

NATIONAL LEARNING CORPORATION

PASSBOOK®

NOTICE

PASSBOOK SERIES®

THE *PASSBOOK SERIES®* has been created to prepare applicants and candidates for the ultimate academic battlefield – the examination room.

At some time in our lives, each and every one of us may be required to take an examination – for validation, matriculation, admission, qualification, registration, certification, or licensure.

Based on the assumption that every applicant or candidate has met the basic formal educational standards, has taken the required number of courses, and read the necessary texts, the *PASSBOOK SERIES®* furnishes the one special preparation which may assure passing with confidence, instead of failing with insecurity. Examination questions – together with answers – are furnished as the basic vehicle for study so that the mysteries of the examination and its compounding difficulties may be eliminated or diminished by a sure method.

This book is meant to help you pass your examination provided that you qualify and are serious in your objective.

The entire field is reviewed through the huge store of content information which is succinctly presented through a provocative and challenging approach – the question-and-answer method.

A climate of success is established by furnishing the correct answers at the end of each test.

You soon learn to recognize types of questions, forms of questions, and patterns of questioning. You may even begin to anticipate expected outcomes.

You perceive that many questions are repeated or adapted so that you can gain acute insights, which may enable you to score many sure points.

You learn how to confront new questions, or types of questions, and to attack them confidently and work out the correct answers.

You note objectives and emphases, and recognize pitfalls and dangers, so that you may make positive educational adjustments.

Moreover, you are kept fully informed in relation to new concepts, methods, practices, and directions in the field.

You discover that you are actually taking the examination all the time: you are preparing for the examination by "taking" an examination, not by reading extraneous and/or supererogatory textbooks.

In short, this PASSBOOK®, used directedly, should be an important factor in helping you to pass your test.

ADMINISTRATIVE ANALYST

DUTIES
Conducts field audits and job evaluations;
Participates in feasibility studies and makes subsequent recommendations;
Participates in cost comparison studies and outlines methods by which recommendation can be effected;
Analyzes budget requests of departments and agencies including capital expenditures;
Analyzes proposals and prepared grant applications for federal or state funded programs;
Maintains a comprehensive inventory of programs financed through federal and state grants;
Develops flow charts and tables of organization; and
Makes recommendations concerning the expanded use of data processing methods.

SCOPE OF THE WRITTEN TEST
The written test will cover knowledge, skills, and/or abilities in such areas as:
1. Administrative analysis;
2. Budgeting;
3. Understanding and interpreting written material;
4. Understanding and interpreting tabular material; and
5. Preparing written material.

HOW TO TAKE A TEST

I. YOU MUST PASS AN EXAMINATION

A. *WHAT EVERY CANDIDATE SHOULD KNOW*

Examination applicants often ask us for help in preparing for the written test. What can I study in advance? What kinds of questions will be asked? How will the test be given? How will the papers be graded?

As an applicant for a civil service examination, you may be wondering about some of these things. Our purpose here is to suggest effective methods of advance study and to describe civil service examinations.

Your chances for success on this examination can be increased if you know how to prepare. Those "pre-examination jitters" can be reduced if you know what to expect. You can even experience an adventure in good citizenship if you know why civil service exams are given.

B. *WHY ARE CIVIL SERVICE EXAMINATIONS GIVEN?*

Civil service examinations are important to you in two ways. As a citizen, you want public jobs filled by employees who know how to do their work. As a job seeker, you want a fair chance to compete for that job on an equal footing with other candidates. The best-known means of accomplishing this two-fold goal is the competitive examination.

Exams are widely publicized throughout the nation. They may be administered for jobs in federal, state, city, municipal, town or village governments or agencies.

Any citizen may apply, with some limitations, such as the age or residence of applicants. Your experience and education may be reviewed to see whether you meet the requirements for the particular examination. When these requirements exist, they are reasonable and applied consistently to all applicants. Thus, a competitive examination may cause you some uneasiness now, but it is your privilege and safeguard.

C. *HOW ARE CIVIL SERVICE EXAMS DEVELOPED?*

Examinations are carefully written by trained technicians who are specialists in the field known as "psychological measurement," in consultation with recognized authorities in the field of work that the test will cover. These experts recommend the subject matter areas or skills to be tested; only those knowledges or skills important to your success on the job are included. The most reliable books and source materials available are used as references. Together, the experts and technicians judge the difficulty level of the questions.

Test technicians know how to phrase questions so that the problem is clearly stated. Their ethics do not permit "trick" or "catch" questions. Questions may have been tried out on sample groups, or subjected to statistical analysis, to determine their usefulness.

Written tests are often used in combination with performance tests, ratings of training and experience, and oral interviews. All of these measures combine to form the best-known means of finding the right person for the right job.

II. HOW TO PASS THE WRITTEN TEST

A. *NATURE OF THE EXAMINATION*

To prepare intelligently for civil service examinations, you should know how they differ from school examinations you have taken. In school you were assigned certain definite pages to read or subjects to cover. The examination questions were quite detailed and usually emphasized memory. Civil service exams, on the other hand, try to discover your present ability to perform the duties of a position, plus your potentiality to learn these duties. In other words, a civil service exam attempts to predict how successful you will be. Questions cover such a broad area that they cannot be as minute and detailed as school exam questions.

In the public service similar kinds of work, or positions, are grouped together in one "class." This process is known as *position-classification*. All the positions in a class are paid according to the salary range for that class. One class title covers all of these positions, and they are all tested by the same examination.

B. *FOUR BASIC STEPS*

1) Study the announcement

How, then, can you know what subjects to study? Our best answer is: "Learn as much as possible about the class of positions for which you've applied." The exam will test the knowledge, skills and abilities needed to do the work.

Your most valuable source of information about the position you want is the official exam announcement. This announcement lists the training and experience qualifications. Check these standards and apply only if you come reasonably close to meeting them.

The brief description of the position in the examination announcement offers some clues to the subjects which will be tested. Think about the job itself. Review the duties in your mind. Can you perform them, or are there some in which you are rusty? Fill in the blank spots in your preparation.

Many jurisdictions preview the written test in the exam announcement by including a section called "Knowledge and Abilities Required," "Scope of the Examination," or some similar heading. Here you will find out specifically what fields will be tested.

2) Review your own background

Once you learn in general what the position is all about, and what you need to know to do the work, ask yourself which subjects you already know fairly well and which need improvement. You may wonder whether to concentrate on improving your strong areas or on building some background in your fields of weakness. When the announcement has specified "some knowledge" or "considerable knowledge," or has used adjectives like "beginning principles of..." or "advanced ... methods," you can get a clue as to the number and difficulty of questions to be asked in any given field. More questions, and hence broader coverage, would be included for those subjects which are more important in the work. Now weigh your strengths and weaknesses against the job requirements and prepare accordingly.

3) Determine the level of the position

Another way to tell how intensively you should prepare is to understand the level of the job for which you are applying. Is it the entering level? In other words, is this the position in which beginners in a field of work are hired? Or is it an intermediate or advanced level? Sometimes this is indicated by such words as "Junior" or "Senior" in the class title. Other jurisdictions use Roman numerals to designate the level – Clerk I, Clerk II, for example. The word "Supervisor" sometimes appears in the title. If the level is not indicated by the title, check the description of duties. Will you be working under very close supervision, or will you have responsibility for independent decisions in this work?

4) Choose appropriate study materials

Now that you know the subjects to be examined and the relative amount of each subject to be covered, you can choose suitable study materials. For beginning level jobs, or even advanced ones, if you have a pronounced weakness in some aspect of your training, read a modern, standard textbook in that field. Be sure it is up to date and has general coverage. Such books are normally available at your library, and the librarian will be glad to help you locate one. For entry-level positions, questions of appropriate difficulty are chosen – neither highly advanced questions, nor those too simple. Such questions require careful thought but not advanced training.

If the position for which you are applying is technical or advanced, you will read more advanced, specialized material. If you are already familiar with the basic principles of your field, elementary textbooks would waste your time. Concentrate on advanced textbooks and technical periodicals. Think through the concepts and review difficult problems in your field.

These are all general sources. You can get more ideas on your own initiative, following these leads. For example, training manuals and publications of the government agency which employs workers in your field can be useful, particularly for technical and professional positions. A letter or visit to the government department involved may result in more specific study suggestions, and certainly will provide you with a more definite idea of the exact nature of the position you are seeking.

III. KINDS OF TESTS

Tests are used for purposes other than measuring knowledge and ability to perform specified duties. For some positions, it is equally important to test ability to make adjustments to new situations or to profit from training. In others, basic mental abilities not dependent on information are essential. Questions which test these things may not appear as pertinent to the duties of the position as those which test for knowledge and information. Yet they are often highly important parts of a fair examination. For very general questions, it is almost impossible to help you direct your study efforts. What we can do is to point out some of the more common of these general abilities needed in public service positions and describe some typical questions.

1) General information

Broad, general information has been found useful for predicting job success in some kinds of work. This is tested in a variety of ways, from vocabulary lists to questions about current events. Basic background in some field of work, such as sociology or economics, may be sampled in a group of questions. Often these are principles which have become familiar to most persons through exposure rather than through formal training. It is difficult to advise you how to study for these questions; being alert to the world around you is our best suggestion.

2) Verbal ability

An example of an ability needed in many positions is verbal or language ability. Verbal ability is, in brief, the ability to use and understand words. Vocabulary and grammar tests are typical measures of this ability. Reading comprehension or paragraph interpretation questions are common in many kinds of civil service tests. You are given a paragraph of written material and asked to find its central meaning.

3) Numerical ability

Number skills can be tested by the familiar arithmetic problem, by checking paired lists of numbers to see which are alike and which are different, or by interpreting charts and graphs. In the latter test, a graph may be printed in the test booklet which you are asked to use as the basis for answering questions.

4) Observation

A popular test for law-enforcement positions is the observation test. A picture is shown to you for several minutes, then taken away. Questions about the picture test your ability to observe both details and larger elements.

5) Following directions

In many positions in the public service, the employee must be able to carry out written instructions dependably and accurately. You may be given a chart with several columns, each column listing a variety of information. The questions require you to carry out directions involving the information given in the chart.

6) Skills and aptitudes

Performance tests effectively measure some manual skills and aptitudes. When the skill is one in which you are trained, such as typing or shorthand, you can practice. These tests are often very much like those given in business school or high school courses. For many of the other skills and aptitudes, however, no short-time preparation can be made. Skills and abilities natural to you or that you have developed throughout your lifetime are being tested.

Many of the general questions just described provide all the data needed to answer the questions and ask you to use your reasoning ability to find the answers. Your best preparation for these tests, as well as for tests of facts and ideas, is to be at your physical and mental best. You, no doubt, have your own methods of getting into an exam-taking mood and keeping "in shape." The next section lists some ideas on this subject.

IV. KINDS OF QUESTIONS

Only rarely is the "essay" question, which you answer in narrative form, used in civil service tests. Civil service tests are usually of the short-answer type. Full instructions for answering these questions will be given to you at the examination. But in case this is your first experience with short-answer questions and separate answer sheets, here is what you need to know:

1) Multiple-choice Questions

Most popular of the short-answer questions is the "multiple choice" or "best answer" question. It can be used, for example, to test for factual knowledge, ability to solve problems or judgment in meeting situations found at work.

A multiple-choice question is normally one of three types—

- It can begin with an incomplete statement followed by several possible endings. You are to find the one ending which *best* completes the statement, although some of the others may not be entirely wrong.
- It can also be a complete statement in the form of a question which is answered by choosing one of the statements listed.
- It can be in the form of a problem – again you select the best answer.

Here is an example of a multiple-choice question with a discussion which should give you some clues as to the method for choosing the right answer:

When an employee has a complaint about his assignment, the action which will *best* help him overcome his difficulty is to

A. discuss his difficulty with his coworkers
B. take the problem to the head of the organization
C. take the problem to the person who gave him the assignment
D. say nothing to anyone about his complaint

In answering this question, you should study each of the choices to find which is best. Consider choice "A" – Certainly an employee may discuss his complaint with fellow employees, but no change or improvement can result, and the complaint remains unresolved. Choice "B" is a poor choice since the head of the organization probably does not know what assignment you have been given, and taking your problem to him is known as "going over the head" of the supervisor. The supervisor, or person who made the assignment, is the person who can clarify it or correct any injustice. Choice "C" is, therefore, correct. To say nothing, as in choice "D," is unwise. Supervisors have and interest in knowing the problems employees are facing, and the employee is seeking a solution to his problem.

2) True/False Questions

The "true/false" or "right/wrong" form of question is sometimes used. Here a complete statement is given. Your job is to decide whether the statement is right or wrong.

SAMPLE: A person-to-person long-distance telephone call costs less than a station-to-station call to the same city.

This statement is wrong, or false, since person-to-person calls are more expensive.

This is not a complete list of all possible question forms, although most of the others are variations of these common types. You will always get complete directions for answering questions. Be sure you understand *how* to mark your answers – ask questions until you do.

V. RECORDING YOUR ANSWERS

For an examination with very few applicants, you may be told to record your answers in the test booklet itself. Separate answer sheets are much more common. If this separate answer sheet is to be scored by machine – and this is often the case – it is highly important that you mark your answers correctly in order to get credit.

An electric scoring machine is often used in civil service offices because of the speed with which papers can be scored. Machine-scored answer sheets must be marked with a pencil, which will be given to you. This pencil has a high graphite content which responds to the electric scoring machine. As a matter of fact, stray dots may register as answers, so do not let your pencil rest on the answer sheet while you are pondering the correct answer. Also, if your pencil lead breaks or is otherwise defective, ask for another.

Since the answer sheet will be dropped in a slot in the scoring machine, be careful not to bend the corners or get the paper crumpled.

The answer sheet normally has five vertical columns of numbers, with 30 numbers to a column. These numbers correspond to the question numbers in your test booklet. After each number, going across the page are four or five pairs of dotted lines. These short dotted lines have small letters or numbers above them. The first two pairs may also have a "T" or "F" above the letters. This indicates that the first two pairs only are to be used if the questions are of the true-false type. If the questions are multiple choice, disregard the "T" and "F" and pay attention only to the small letters or numbers.

Answer your questions in the manner of the sample that follows:

32. The largest city in the United States is
    A. Washington, D.C.
    B. New York City
    C. Chicago
    D. Detroit
    E. San Francisco

1) Choose the answer you think is best. (New York City is the largest, so "B" is correct.)
2) Find the row of dotted lines numbered the same as the question you are answering. (Find row number 32)
3) Find the pair of dotted lines corresponding to the answer. (Find the pair of lines under the mark "B.")
4) Make a solid black mark between the dotted lines.

VI. BEFORE THE TEST

Common sense will help you find procedures to follow to get ready for an examination. Too many of us, however, overlook these sensible measures. Indeed, nervousness and fatigue have been found to be the most serious reasons why applicants fail to do their best on civil service tests. Here is a list of reminders:

- Begin your preparation early – Don't wait until the last minute to go scurrying around for books and materials or to find out what the position is all about.
- Prepare continuously – An hour a night for a week is better than an all-night cram session. This has been definitely established. What is more, a night a

week for a month will return better dividends than crowding your study into a shorter period of time.

- Locate the place of the exam – You have been sent a notice telling you when and where to report for the examination. If the location is in a different town or otherwise unfamiliar to you, it would be well to inquire the best route and learn something about the building.
- Relax the night before the test – Allow your mind to rest. Do not study at all that night. Plan some mild recreation or diversion; then go to bed early and get a good night's sleep.
- Get up early enough to make a leisurely trip to the place for the test – This way unforeseen events, traffic snarls, unfamiliar buildings, etc. will not upset you.
- Dress comfortably – A written test is not a fashion show. You will be known by number and not by name, so wear something comfortable.
- Leave excess paraphernalia at home – Shopping bags and odd bundles will get in your way. You need bring only the items mentioned in the official notice you received; usually everything you need is provided. Do not bring reference books to the exam. They will only confuse those last minutes and be taken away from you when in the test room.
- Arrive somewhat ahead of time – If because of transportation schedules you must get there very early, bring a newspaper or magazine to take your mind off yourself while waiting.
- Locate the examination room – When you have found the proper room, you will be directed to the seat or part of the room where you will sit. Sometimes you are given a sheet of instructions to read while you are waiting. Do not fill out any forms until you are told to do so; just read them and be prepared.
- Relax and prepare to listen to the instructions
- If you have any physical problem that may keep you from doing your best, be sure to tell the test administrator. If you are sick or in poor health, you really cannot do your best on the exam. You can come back and take the test some other time.

VII. AT THE TEST

The day of the test is here and you have the test booklet in your hand. The temptation to get going is very strong. Caution! There is more to success than knowing the right answers. You must know how to identify your papers and understand variations in the type of short-answer question used in this particular examination. Follow these suggestions for maximum results from your efforts:

1) Cooperate with the monitor

The test administrator has a duty to create a situation in which you can be as much at ease as possible. He will give instructions, tell you when to begin, check to see that you are marking your answer sheet correctly, and so on. He is not there to guard you, although he will see that your competitors do not take unfair advantage. He wants to help you do your best.

2) Listen to all instructions

Don't jump the gun! Wait until you understand all directions. In most civil service tests you get more time than you need to answer the questions. So don't be in a hurry.

Read each word of instructions until you clearly understand the meaning. Study the examples, listen to all announcements and follow directions. Ask questions if you do not understand what to do.

3) Identify your papers

Civil service exams are usually identified by number only. You will be assigned a number; you must not put your name on your test papers. Be sure to copy your number correctly. Since more than one exam may be given, copy your exact examination title.

4) Plan your time

Unless you are told that a test is a "speed" or "rate of work" test, speed itself is usually not important. Time enough to answer all the questions will be provided, but this does not mean that you have all day. An overall time limit has been set. Divide the total time (in minutes) by the number of questions to determine the approximate time you have for each question.

5) Do not linger over difficult questions

If you come across a difficult question, mark it with a paper clip (useful to have along) and come back to it when you have been through the booklet. One caution if you do this – be sure to skip a number on your answer sheet as well. Check often to be sure that you have not lost your place and that you are marking in the row numbered the same as the question you are answering.

6) Read the questions

Be sure you know what the question asks! Many capable people are unsuccessful because they failed to *read* the questions correctly.

7) Answer all questions

Unless you have been instructed that a penalty will be deducted for incorrect answers, it is better to guess than to omit a question.

8) Speed tests

It is often better NOT to guess on speed tests. It has been found that on timed tests people are tempted to spend the last few seconds before time is called in marking answers at random – without even reading them – in the hope of picking up a few extra points. To discourage this practice, the instructions may warn you that your score will be "corrected" for guessing. That is, a penalty will be applied. The incorrect answers will be deducted from the correct ones, or some other penalty formula will be used.

9) Review your answers

If you finish before time is called, go back to the questions you guessed or omitted to give them further thought. Review other answers if you have time.

10) Return your test materials

If you are ready to leave before others have finished or time is called, take ALL your materials to the monitor and leave quietly. Never take any test material with you. The monitor can discover whose papers are not complete, and taking a test booklet may be grounds for disqualification.

VIII. EXAMINATION TECHNIQUES

1) Read the general instructions carefully. These are usually printed on the first page of the exam booklet. As a rule, these instructions refer to the timing of the examination; the fact that you should not start work until the signal and must stop work at a signal, etc. If there are any *special* instructions, such as a choice of questions to be answered, make sure that you note this instruction carefully.

2) When you are ready to start work on the examination, that is as soon as the signal has been given, read the instructions to each question booklet, underline any key words or phrases, such as *least, best, outline, describe* and the like. In this way you will tend to answer as requested rather than discover on reviewing your paper that you *listed without describing*, that you selected the *worst* choice rather than the *best* choice, etc.

3) If the examination is of the objective or multiple-choice type – that is, each question will also give a series of possible answers: A, B, C or D, and you are called upon to select the best answer and write the letter next to that answer on your answer paper – it is advisable to start answering each question in turn. There may be anywhere from 50 to 100 such questions in the three or four hours allotted and you can see how much time would be taken if you read through all the questions before beginning to answer any. Furthermore, if you come across a question or group of questions which you know would be difficult to answer, it would undoubtedly affect your handling of all the other questions.

4) If the examination is of the essay type and contains but a few questions, it is a moot point as to whether you should read all the questions before starting to answer any one. Of course, if you are given a choice – say five out of seven and the like – then it is essential to read all the questions so you can eliminate the two that are most difficult. If, however, you are asked to answer all the questions, there may be danger in trying to answer the easiest one first because you may find that you will spend too much time on it. The best technique is to answer the first question, then proceed to the second, etc.

5) Time your answers. Before the exam begins, write down the time it started, then add the time allowed for the examination and write down the time it must be completed, then divide the time available somewhat as follows:
   - If 3-1/2 hours are allowed, that would be 210 minutes. If you have 80 objective-type questions, that would be an average of 2-1/2 minutes per question. Allow yourself no more than 2 minutes per question, or a total of 160 minutes, which will permit about 50 minutes to review.
   - If for the time allotment of 210 minutes there are 7 essay questions to answer, that would average about 30 minutes a question. Give yourself only 25 minutes per question so that you have about 35 minutes to review.

6) The most important instruction is to *read each question* and make sure you know what is wanted. The second most important instruction is to *time yourself properly* so that you answer every question. The third most

important instruction is to *answer every question.* Guess if you have to but include something for each question. Remember that you will receive no credit for a blank and will probably receive some credit if you write something in answer to an essay question. If you guess a letter – say "B" for a multiple-choice question – you may have guessed right. If you leave a blank as an answer to a multiple-choice question, the examiners may respect your feelings but it will not add a point to your score. Some exams may penalize you for wrong answers, so in such cases *only*, you may not want to guess unless you have some basis for your answer.

7) Suggestions
   a. Objective-type questions
      1. Examine the question booklet for proper sequence of pages and questions
      2. Read all instructions carefully
      3. Skip any question which seems too difficult; return to it after all other questions have been answered
      4. Apportion your time properly; do not spend too much time on any single question or group of questions
      5. Note and underline key words – *all, most, fewest, least, best, worst, same, opposite,* etc.
      6. Pay particular attention to negatives
      7. Note unusual option, e.g., unduly long, short, complex, different or similar in content to the body of the question
      8. Observe the use of "hedging" words – *probably, may, most likely,* etc.
      9. Make sure that your answer is put next to the same number as the question
      10. Do not second-guess unless you have good reason to believe the second answer is definitely more correct
      11. Cross out original answer if you decide another answer is more accurate; do not erase until you are ready to hand your paper in
      12. Answer all questions; guess unless instructed otherwise
      13. Leave time for review

   b. Essay questions
      1. Read each question carefully
      2. Determine exactly what is wanted. Underline key words or phrases.
      3. Decide on outline or paragraph answer
      4. Include many different points and elements unless asked to develop any one or two points or elements
      5. Show impartiality by giving pros and cons unless directed to select one side only
      6. Make and write down any assumptions you find necessary to answer the questions
      7. Watch your English, grammar, punctuation and choice of words
      8. Time your answers; don't crowd material

8) Answering the essay question

Most essay questions can be answered by framing the specific response around several key words or ideas. Here are a few such key words or ideas:

M's: manpower, materials, methods, money, management

P's: purpose, program, policy, plan, procedure, practice, problems, pitfalls, personnel, public relations

    a. Six basic steps in handling problems:
1. Preliminary plan and background development
2. Collect information, data and facts
3. Analyze and interpret information, data and facts
4. Analyze and develop solutions as well as make recommendations
5. Prepare report and sell recommendations
6. Install recommendations and follow up effectiveness

    b. Pitfalls to avoid
1. *Taking things for granted* – A statement of the situation does not necessarily imply that each of the elements is necessarily true; for example, a complaint may be invalid and biased so that all that can be taken for granted is that a complaint has been registered
2. *Considering only one side of a situation* – Wherever possible, indicate several alternatives and then point out the reasons you selected the best one
3. *Failing to indicate follow up* – Whenever your answer indicates action on your part, make certain that you will take proper follow-up action to see how successful your recommendations, procedures or actions turn out to be
4. *Taking too long in answering any single question* – Remember to time your answers properly

IX. AFTER THE TEST

Scoring procedures differ in detail among civil service jurisdictions although the general principles are the same. Whether the papers are hand-scored or graded by machine we have described, they are nearly always graded by number. That is, the person who marks the paper knows only the number – never the name – of the applicant. Not until all the papers have been graded will they be matched with names. If other tests, such as training and experience or oral interview ratings have been given, scores will be combined. Different parts of the examination usually have different weights. For example, the written test might count 60 percent of the final grade, and a rating of training and experience 40 percent. In many jurisdictions, veterans will have a certain number of points added to their grades.

After the final grade has been determined, the names are placed in grade order and an eligible list is established. There are various methods for resolving ties between those who get the same final grade – probably the most common is to place first the name of the person whose application was received first. Job offers are made from the eligible list in the order the names appear on it. You will be notified of your grade and your rank as soon as all these computations have been made. This will be done as rapidly as possible.

People who are found to meet the requirements in the announcement are called "eligibles." Their names are put on a list of eligible candidates. An eligible's chances of getting a job depend on how high he stands on this list and how fast agencies are filling jobs from the list.

When a job is to be filled from a list of eligibles, the agency asks for the names of people on the list of eligibles for that job. When the civil service commission receives this request, it sends to the agency the names of the three people highest on this list. Or, if the job to be filled has specialized requirements, the office sends the agency the names of the top three persons who meet these requirements from the general list.

The appointing officer makes a choice from among the three people whose names were sent to him. If the selected person accepts the appointment, the names of the others are put back on the list to be considered for future openings.

That is the rule in hiring from all kinds of eligible lists, whether they are for typist, carpenter, chemist, or something else. For every vacancy, the appointing officer has his choice of any one of the top three eligibles on the list. This explains why the person whose name is on top of the list sometimes does not get an appointment when some of the persons lower on the list do. If the appointing officer chooses the second or third eligible, the No. 1 eligible does not get a job at once, but stays on the list until he is appointed or the list is terminated.

X. HOW TO PASS THE INTERVIEW TEST

The examination for which you applied requires an oral interview test. You have already taken the written test and you are now being called for the interview test – the final part of the formal examination.

You may think that it is not possible to prepare for an interview test and that there are no procedures to follow during an interview. Our purpose is to point out some things you can do in advance that will help you and some good rules to follow and pitfalls to avoid while you are being interviewed.

What is an interview supposed to test?

The written examination is designed to test the technical knowledge and competence of the candidate; the oral is designed to evaluate intangible qualities, not readily measured otherwise, and to establish a list showing the relative fitness of each candidate – as measured against his competitors – for the position sought. Scoring is not on the basis of "right" and "wrong," but on a sliding scale of values ranging from "not passable" to "outstanding." As a matter of fact, it is possible to achieve a relatively low score without a single "incorrect" answer because of evident weakness in the qualities being measured.

Occasionally, an examination may consist entirely of an oral test – either an individual or a group oral. In such cases, information is sought concerning the technical knowledges and abilities of the candidate, since there has been no written examination for this purpose. More commonly, however, an oral test is used to supplement a written examination.

Who conducts interviews?

The composition of oral boards varies among different jurisdictions. In nearly all, a representative of the personnel department serves as chairman. One of the members of the board may be a representative of the department in which the candidate would work. In some cases, "outside experts" are used, and, frequently, a businessman or some other representative of the general public is asked to serve. Labor and management or other special groups may be represented. The aim is to secure the services of experts in the appropriate field.

However the board is composed, it is a good idea (and not at all improper or unethical) to ascertain in advance of the interview who the members are and what groups they represent. When you are introduced to them, you will have some idea of their backgrounds and interests, and at least you will not stutter and stammer over their names.

What should be done before the interview?

While knowledge about the board members is useful and takes some of the surprise element out of the interview, there is other preparation which is more substantive. It *is* possible to prepare for an oral interview – in several ways:

1) Keep a copy of your application and review it carefully before the interview

This may be the only document before the oral board, and the starting point of the interview. Know what education and experience you have listed there, and the sequence and dates of all of it. Sometimes the board will ask you to review the highlights of your experience for them; you should not have to hem and haw doing it.

2) Study the class specification and the examination announcement

Usually, the oral board has one or both of these to guide them. The qualities, characteristics or knowledges required by the position sought are stated in these documents. They offer valuable clues as to the nature of the oral interview. For example, if the job involves supervisory responsibilities, the announcement will usually indicate that knowledge of modern supervisory methods and the qualifications of the candidate as a supervisor will be tested. If so, you can expect such questions, frequently in the form of a hypothetical situation which you are expected to solve. NEVER go into an oral without knowledge of the duties and responsibilities of the job you seek.

3) Think through each qualification required

Try to visualize the kind of questions you would ask if you were a board member. How well could you answer them? Try especially to appraise your own knowledge and background in each area, *measured against the job sought*, and identify any areas in which you are weak. Be critical and realistic – do not flatter yourself.

4) Do some general reading in areas in which you feel you may be weak

For example, if the job involves supervision and your past experience has NOT, some general reading in supervisory methods and practices, particularly in the field of human relations, might be useful. Do NOT study agency procedures or detailed manuals. The oral board will be testing your understanding and capacity, not your memory.

5) Get a good night's sleep and watch your general health and mental attitude

You will want a clear head at the interview. Take care of a cold or any other minor ailment, and of course, no hangovers.

What should be done on the day of the interview?

Now comes the day of the interview itself. Give yourself plenty of time to get there. Plan to arrive somewhat ahead of the scheduled time, particularly if your appointment is in the fore part of the day. If a previous candidate fails to appear, the board might be ready for you a bit early. By early afternoon an oral board is almost invariably behind schedule if there are many candidates, and you may have to wait.

Take along a book or magazine to read, or your application to review, but leave any extraneous material in the waiting room when you go in for your interview. In any event, relax and compose yourself.

The matter of dress is important. The board is forming impressions about you – from your experience, your manners, your attitude, and your appearance. Give your personal appearance careful attention. Dress your best, but not your flashiest. Choose conservative, appropriate clothing, and be sure it is immaculate. This is a business interview, and your appearance should indicate that you regard it as such. Besides, being well groomed and properly dressed will help boost your confidence.

Sooner or later, someone will call your name and escort you into the interview room. *This is it.* From here on you are on your own. It is too late for any more preparation. But remember, you asked for this opportunity to prove your fitness, and you are here because your request was granted.

What happens when you go in?

The usual sequence of events will be as follows: The clerk (who is often the board stenographer) will introduce you to the chairman of the oral board, who will introduce you to the other members of the board. Acknowledge the introductions before you sit down. Do not be surprised if you find a microphone facing you or a stenotypist sitting by. Oral interviews are usually recorded in the event of an appeal or other review.

Usually the chairman of the board will open the interview by reviewing the highlights of your education and work experience from your application – primarily for the benefit of the other members of the board, as well as to get the material into the record. Do not interrupt or comment unless there is an error or significant misinterpretation; if that is the case, do not hesitate. But do not quibble about insignificant matters. Also, he will usually ask you some question about your education, experience or your present job – partly to get you to start talking and to establish the interviewing "rapport." He may start the actual questioning, or turn it over to one of the other members. Frequently, each member undertakes the questioning on a particular area, one in which he is perhaps most competent, so you can expect each member to participate in the examination. Because time is limited, you may also expect some rather abrupt switches in the direction the questioning takes, so do not be upset by it. Normally, a board member will not pursue a single line of questioning unless he discovers a particular strength or weakness.

After each member has participated, the chairman will usually ask whether any member has any further questions, then will ask you if you have anything you wish to add. Unless you are expecting this question, it may floor you. Worse, it may start you off on an extended, extemporaneous speech. The board is not usually seeking more information. The question is principally to offer you a last opportunity to present further qualifications or to indicate that you have nothing to add. So, if you feel that a significant qualification or characteristic has been overlooked, it is proper to point it out in a sentence or so. Do not compliment the board on the thoroughness of their examination – they have been sketchy, and you know it. If you wish, merely say, "No thank you, I have nothing further to add." This is a point where you can "talk yourself out" of a good impression or fail to present an important bit of information. Remember, *you close the interview yourself.*

The chairman will then say, "That is all, Mr. _____, thank you." Do not be startled; the interview is over, and quicker than you think. Thank him, gather your belongings and take your leave. Save your sigh of relief for the other side of the door.

How to put your best foot forward

Throughout this entire process, you may feel that the board individually and collectively is trying to pierce your defenses, seek out your hidden weaknesses and embarrass and confuse you. Actually, this is not true. They are obliged to make an appraisal of your qualifications for the job you are seeking, and they want to see you in your best light. Remember, they must interview all candidates and a non-cooperative candidate may become a failure in spite of their best efforts to bring out his qualifications. Here are 15 suggestions that will help you:

1) Be natural – Keep your attitude confident, not cocky

If you are not confident that you can do the job, do not expect the board to be. Do not apologize for your weaknesses, try to bring out your strong points. The board is interested in a positive, not negative, presentation. Cockiness will antagonize any board member and make him wonder if you are covering up a weakness by a false show of strength.

2) Get comfortable, but don't lounge or sprawl

Sit erectly but not stiffly. A careless posture may lead the board to conclude that you are careless in other things, or at least that you are not impressed by the importance of the occasion. Either conclusion is natural, even if incorrect. Do not fuss with your clothing, a pencil or an ashtray. Your hands may occasionally be useful to emphasize a point; do not let them become a point of distraction.

3) Do not wisecrack or make small talk

This is a serious situation, and your attitude should show that you consider it as such. Further, the time of the board is limited – they do not want to waste it, and neither should you.

4) Do not exaggerate your experience or abilities

In the first place, from information in the application or other interviews and sources, the board may know more about you than you think. Secondly, you probably will not get away with it. An experienced board is rather adept at spotting such a situation, so do not take the chance.

5) If you know a board member, do not make a point of it, yet do not hide it

Certainly you are not fooling him, and probably not the other members of the board. Do not try to take advantage of your acquaintanceship – it will probably do you little good.

6) Do not dominate the interview

Let the board do that. They will give you the clues – do not assume that you have to do all the talking. Realize that the board has a number of questions to ask you, and do not try to take up all the interview time by showing off your extensive knowledge of the answer to the first one.

7) Be attentive

You only have 20 minutes or so, and you should keep your attention at its sharpest throughout. When a member is addressing a problem or question to you, give him your undivided attention. Address your reply principally to him, but do not exclude the other board members.

8) Do not interrupt

A board member may be stating a problem for you to analyze. He will ask you a question when the time comes. Let him state the problem, and wait for the question.

9) Make sure you understand the question

Do not try to answer until you are sure what the question is. If it is not clear, restate it in your own words or ask the board member to clarify it for you. However, do not haggle about minor elements.

10) Reply promptly but not hastily

A common entry on oral board rating sheets is "candidate responded readily," or "candidate hesitated in replies." Respond as promptly and quickly as you can, but do not jump to a hasty, ill-considered answer.

11) Do not be peremptory in your answers

A brief answer is proper – but do not fire your answer back. That is a losing game from your point of view. The board member can probably ask questions much faster than you can answer them.

12) Do not try to create the answer you think the board member wants

He is interested in what kind of mind you have and how it works – not in playing games. Furthermore, he can usually spot this practice and will actually grade you down on it.

13) Do not switch sides in your reply merely to agree with a board member

Frequently, a member will take a contrary position merely to draw you out and to see if you are willing and able to defend your point of view. Do not start a debate, yet do not surrender a good position. If a position is worth taking, it is worth defending.

14) Do not be afraid to admit an error in judgment if you are shown to be wrong

The board knows that you are forced to reply without any opportunity for careful consideration. Your answer may be demonstrably wrong. If so, admit it and get on with the interview.

15) Do not dwell at length on your present job

The opening question may relate to your present assignment. Answer the question but do not go into an extended discussion. You are being examined for a *new* job, not your present one. As a matter of fact, try to phrase ALL your answers in terms of the job for which you are being examined.

Basis of Rating

Probably you will forget most of these "do's" and "don'ts" when you walk into the oral interview room. Even remembering them all will not ensure you a passing grade. Perhaps you did not have the qualifications in the first place. But remembering them will help you to put your best foot forward, without treading on the toes of the board members.

Rumor and popular opinion to the contrary notwithstanding, an oral board wants you to make the best appearance possible. They know you are under pressure – but they also want to see how you respond to it as a guide to what your reaction would be under the pressures of the job you seek. They will be influenced by the degree of poise you display, the personal traits you show and the manner in which you respond.

EXAMINATION SECTION

EXAMINATION SECTION
TEST 1

DIRECTIONS: Each question or incomplete statement is followed by several suggested answers or completions. Select the one that BEST answers the question or completes the statement. *PRINT THE LETTER OF THE CORRECT ANSWER IN THE SPACE AT THE RIGHT.*

1. Of the following factors, which one is LEAST important in determining the size of staff needed in conducting an organization survey?
   The
   A. effectiveness of the personnel in supplying data for the study
   B. extent of report writing anticipated
   C. number of field locations and headquarters staff units to be covered
   D. number of individuals to be interviewed as part of fact finding

   1.___

2. In planning a systems survey, which one of the following is MOST important in carrying out an effective survey after the purpose and scope of the survey has been determined?
   The
   A. format of the survey report
   B. methods and techniques to be employed
   C. personality problems which may materialize
   D. exact starting and completion dates

   2.___

3. Which of the following is the BEST way of organizing a final report?
   A. Begin and end the report with a summary of conclusions showing how conclusions were changed as a result of findings and recommendations
   B. Begin the report with an overall summary and then place findings and recommendations in several sections
   C. Intertwine findings and conclusions in such a manner as to make the report readable and interesting
   D. Place the findings and recommendations in separate sections avoiding conclusions to the maximum extent possible

   3.___

4. Which of the following disadvantages is the MOST serious in making reports verbally rather than in writing?
   A. An effective analyst may not be a good public speaker.
   B. Verbal reports are conveniently forgotten.
   C. It may not generate actions and follow-through by recipients.
   D. There is a lack of permanent record to which one may later refer.

   4.___

5. Following a management survey, which of the following   5.__
represents the MOST serious pitfall which may be made in
recommending improvements?
   A. Failure to convince people of the benefits to be
      derived from the recommendations
   B. Failure to freely discuss recommendations with those
      who must live with them
   C. Tendency of the survey team to put their own persona-
      lities into the report
   D. Tendency to deal in personalities instead of dealing
      with objectives and sound management practices

6. A working outline for management analysts should include   6.__
all of the following EXCEPT
   A. a chronological outline of the work steps
   B. a determination of background information needed
   C. the distribution of outline to key staff and line
      personnel
   D. preliminary conclusions

7. Which one of the following areas is the MOST critical for   7.__
an analyst during the fact-finding stage of a study?
   A. Accuracy of data appearing in reports
   B. Attitude of those being interviewed by the analyst
   C. Observations and tentative conclusions reached by
      the analyst
   D. Suggestions and recommendations of interviewees

8. Creating an organization embraces all of the following   8.__
areas of management EXCEPT
   A. clarification of objectives
   B. determining the number of people required to man the
      organization
   C. establishing operating budgets to make the plan
      effective
   D. proper structuring of all key positions

9. In an organization, the MAJOR barrier to accepting change   9.__
is the
   A. assumption by management that everyone will willingly
      accept change
   B. failure by management to present proposed changes in
      a proper fashion
   C. lack of adaptive abilities on the part of employees
   D. lack of understanding on the part of employees of
      sound management principles

10. A supervisor who wishes to attain established objectives   10.__
should concentrate on
   A. determining whether management is operating at
      maximum effectiveness
   B. making suggestions for improving the organization
   C. planning work assignments
   D. securing salary increases for needy employees

11. A usually competent employee complains that he does not   11.___
    understand the procedures to be followed in performing a
    certain task although the supervisor has explained them
    twice and has demonstrated them.
    Of the following, the BEST course of action for the super-
    visor to take is to
    A. ask the employee whether he has any problems which
       are bothering him
    B. assign someone else to the job
    C. explain the procedures again and demonstrate at the
       same time
    D. have the employee perform the job while he watches
       and gives additional instructions

12. GENERALLY, in order to be completely qualified as a   12.___
    supervisor, a person
    A. should be able to perform exceptionally well at least
       one of the jobs he supervises and have some knowledge
       of the others
    B. must have an intimate working knowledge of all facets
       of the jobs which he supervises
    C. should know the basic principles and procedures of
       the jobs he supervises
    D. need know little or nothing of the jobs which he
       supervises as long as he knows the principles of
       supervision

13. Which of the following contributes MOST to the problem of   13.___
    waste and inefficiency in offices?
    A. Cost control is a budget function primarily.
    B. Most organizations do not have soundly conceived
       budgets.
    C. Procedures improvement staffs have not as yet gained
       acceptance among white collar workers.
    D. Supervisors generally are uninterested in making
       improvements.

14. Which of the following contributes MOST to the great   14.___
    number of duplicate reports and double-checking procedures
    frequently found in offices?
    The
    A. desire for protection
    B. desire to improve problem solving
    C. intent to *manage by exception*
    D. need for budget data

15. Which one of the following BEST identifies the narrow   15.___
    technician as compared with the broad-gauged analyst?
    He
    A. analyzes the activities of an agency
    B. attempts to form sound relationships with departmental
       personnel
    C. focuses attention on forms design and appearance
    D. follows work flow from one bureau to another by
       charting operational steps

16. The percentage of budget funds allocated to fixed overhead   16.__
    costs can be MOST effectively reduced by
    A. a soundly conceived *promotion from within* policy
    B. increasing the amount of work performed
    C. relocating to areas closer to the center of cities
    D. tightening the *fixed cost* portion of the budget

17. The term *span of control* USUALLY refers to   17.__
    A. individuals reporting to a common supervisor
    B. individuals with whom one individual has contact in
      the course of performing his assigned duties
    C. levels of supervision in an organization
    D. percentage of time in an organization devoted to
      supervisory duties

18. For an analyst, which of the following is generally LEAST   18.__
    important in conducting a management survey?
    A. Ability of employees to understand goals of the survey
    B. Attitude of supervisors of employees
    C. Availability of employees for interviews
    D. Cooperation of employees

19. Of the following, morale in an agency is generally MOST   19.__
    significantly affected by
    A. agency policies and procedures
    B. agency recognition of executives supporting agency
      goals
    C. the extent to which an agency meets its announced
      goals
    D. the number of management surveys conducted in an
      agency

20. Which of the following BEST describes the principle of   20.__
    management by exception?
    A. Allocating executive time and effort in direct rela-
      tion to the dollar values of the budget
    B. Decentralizing management and dealing primarily with
      problem areas
    C. Measuring only direct costs
    D. Setting goals and objectives and managing only these

21. A WEAKNESS of many budgetary systems today is that they   21.__
    A. are subjectively determined by those most directly
      involved
    B. focus on management weakness rather than management
      strength
    C. only show variable costs
    D. show in detail why losses are occurring

22. Standards on which budgets are developed should be based   22.__
    PRIMARILY on
    A. a general consensus   B. agency wishes
    C. analytical studies   D. historical performance

23. The income, cost, and expense goals making up a budget
are aimed at achieving a predetermined objective but do
not necessarily measure the lowest possible costs.
This is PRIMARILY so because
    A. budget committees are accounting-oriented and are
not sympathetic with the supervisor's personnel
problems
    B. budget committees fail to recognize the difference
between direct and indirect costs
    C. the level of expenditures provided for in a budget
by budget committees is frequently an arbitrary
rather than a scientifically determined amount
    D. budget committees spend considerable time evaluating
data to the point that the material gathered is not
representative or current

23.___

24. Linear programming has all of the following characteristics EXCEPT: It
    A. is concerned with an optimum position in relation to
some objective
    B. involves the selection among alternatives or the
appropriate combination of alternatives
    C. not only requires that variables be qualitative but
also rests on the assumption that the relations among
the variables are minimized
    D. takes into account constraints or limits within which
the decision is to be reached

24.___

25. In the PERT planning system, the time in which a non-
critical task can slip schedule without holding up a
project is USUALLY called
    A. constraint   B. duration time
    C. dead time   D. float or slack

25.___

26. The Produc-trol board and Schedugraphs are commercial
variations of the _____ chart.
    A. flow   B. Gantt
    C. layout   D. multiple activity

26.___

27. The item which cannot be analyzed by such schematic
techniques as the frequency polygon and the histogram
is the
    A. age of accounts receivable
    B. morale and cohesiveness of work groups
    C. number of accidents in a plant
    D. wage pattern

27.___

28. An essential employee benefit of work measurement which
FREQUENTLY is the key to the successful implementation
of such a program is
    A. equitable work distribution
    B. facilitation of the development of budgets
    C. measurement and control of office productivity
    D. prevention of unfair work distribution

28.___

29. An organizational arrangement whereby different employees perform different work steps upon the same work items at the same time is called the _____ method.
    A. functional
    B. homogenous
    C. parallel or linear arrangement
    D. unit assembly

29.___

30. Frequently, opposition to a management survey stems from an executive's feeling that he might be considered responsible for the unsatisfactory conditions that the project is aimed at correcting.
    To overcome this type of opposition, the analyst should GENERALLY
    A. avoid the issue altogether
    B. face the situation *head on* and, if the executive is responsible, tell him so
    C. offer a reasonable explanation for those conditions early enough in the discussion to forestall any implication of criticism
    D. place the blame for the unsatisfactory conditions at the lowest level in the organization to avoid incriminating the boss

30.___

31. Which of the following situations is LEAST likely to require a management survey?
    A. Changes in policy
    B. Management requests for additional manpower
    C. Legislation mandating changes in operating procedures
    D. Significantly lower costs than anticipated

31.___

32. The efficiency of a procedure is often influenced by the practices or performance of departments that play no direct part in carrying it out.
    In view of this, the analyst must
    A. disregard the practices or performance of departments that play no direct part in the procedure
    B. do the very best job within the department studied to compensate for the outside problems
    C. ask for assistance in solving the problems created by this situation
    D. study and evaluate the external factors to the extent that they bear on the problem

32.___

33. Which one of the following is NOT a key step in staff delegation and development?
    A. Evaluation of the completed job
    B. Preparation of a subordinate to accept additional duties
    C. Review of daily progress
    D. Selection of a suitable job to be delegated

33.___

34. Which one of the following is NOT an essential charac-　　34.___
teristic of effective delegation?
   A. In delegating, the supervisor is no longer responsible.
   B. The individual to whom authority is delegated must
be accountable for fulfillment of the task.
   C. The individual to whom authority is delegated must
clearly understand this authority.
   D. The individual to whom authority is delegated must
get honest recognition for a job well done.

35. Whenever a manager must determine how long an operation　35.___
should take, he is involved with the problem of setting
a time standard.
To PROPERLY set time standards, the manager must distin-
guish between
   A. estimation processes and evaluation processes
   B. performance of the slowest employee and performance
of the fastest employee
   C. stop watch study and work sampling
   D. synthetic and arbitrary systems

36. Assuming a report is needed, which approach USUALLY　　36.___
facilitates implementation?
A
   A. draft report submitted to key people for review,
discussion, modification, and then resubmission in
final form
   B. report in final form which sets forth alternate
recommended solutions
   C. report which sets forth the problems and the
recommended solution in conformance with the desires
of those most directly involved
   D. visual presentation with minimal report writing

37. Of the following elements, which is the LEAST important　37.___
in writing a survey report?
A
   A. definite course of action to be followed
   B. listing of benefits to be gained through implementa-
tion
   C. review of opinions as differentiated from facts
   D. summary of conclusions

38. Physical appearance and accuracy are important features　38.___
in gaining acceptance to recommendations. Which one of
the following might be OVERLOOKED in preparing a report
which is to have wide distribution?
   A. A comprehensive index
   B. An attractive binder
   C. Proper spacing and page layout
   D. Charts and tables

39. The elimination of meaningless reports, although reducing 39.___
the total information output, IMPROVES the management
process by
A. determining the number of employees required to
perform the work assigned
B. identifying the difference between direct and indirect costs
C. increasing the effectiveness of executives
D. limiting the budget to variable costs

40. In determining whether or not to use a computerized 40.___
system as opposed to a manual system, which of the
following would normally have the MOST influence on
the decision?
The
A. availability of analysts and programmers to design
and install the system
B. availability of computer time
C. basic premise that all computerized systems are
superior to manual systems
D. volume and complexity of transactions required

KEY (CORRECT ANSWERS)

1. A	11. D	21. A	31. D
2. B	12. C	22. C	32. D
3. B	13. C	23. C	33. C
4. D	14. A	24. C	34. A
5. D	15. C	25. D	35. A
6. D	16. B	26. B	36. A
7. C	17. A	27. B	37. C
8. C	18. A	28. A	38. B
9. B	19. A	29. D	39. C
10. C	20. B	30. C	40. D

TEST 2

DIRECTIONS: Each question or incomplete statement is followed by several suggested answers or completions. Select the one that BEST answers the question or completes the statement. *PRINT THE LETTER OF THE CORRECT ANSWER IN THE SPACE AT THE RIGHT.*

1. The one of the following that is NOT normally involved in the development of a management information system is
    A. determination of the best method of preparing and presenting the required information
    B. determination of line and staff relationships within the various units of the organizational structure
    C. determination of what specific information is needed for decision-making and control
    D. identification of the critical aspects of the business, i.e., the end results and other elements of performance which need to be planned and controlled

1.____

2. The long-term growth in size and complexity of both business and government has increased management's dependence on more formal written summaries of operating results in place of the informal, on-the-spot observations and judgments of smaller organizations.
In addition, there is a growing management need to
    A. increase the complexity of those phases of the management process which have previously been simplified
    B. increase the speed and accuracy of giant computers
    C. measure the effectiveness of managerial performance
    D. reduce alcoholism by greatly limiting personal contacts between the various levels of management within the organization

2.____

3. Of the following, it is MOST essential that a management information system provide information needed for
    A. determining computer time requirements
    B. developing new office layouts
    C. drawing new organization charts
    D. planning and measuring results

3.____

4. The PRIMARY purpose of control reports is to
    A. compare actual performance with planned results
    B. determine staffing requirements
    C. determine the work flow
    D. develop a new budget

4.____

5. Which one of the following has the GREATEST negative impact on communications in a large organization?
    A. Delays in formulating variable policies relating to communications

5.____

B. Failure to conduct comprehensive courses in communications skills
C. Failure to get information to those who need it
D. Unclear organizational objectives

6. Major random access devices for a computer include all of the following EXCEPT
    A. magnetic disks   B. magnetic drums
    C. magnetic plastic tapes   D. mass storage devices
6.___

7. The type of computer configuration in which the data are processed at one time after they have been made a matter of record is known as
    A. batching   B. in line   C. off line   D. real time
7.___

8. A computer configuration system in which the input or output equipment is directly connected and operates under control of the computer is known as
    A. off line   B. on line
    C. random access   D. real time
8.___

9. The PRINCIPAL distinction between a digital computer and an analogue computer is one
    A. counts while the other measures electrical current
    B. is an IBM monopoly while the other is a Remington-Rand monopoly
    C. is used primarily in manufacturing while the other is used primarily for billing
    D. system is based on cards while the other is based on discs
9.___

10. All digital computers are generally considered to consist of four major sections.
The one of the following which is NOT a major section is
    A. buffer   B. control
    C. processing   D. storage
10.___

11. Of the following, administrative control is PRIMARILY dependent upon
    A. adequate information
    B. a widespread spy network
    C. strict supervisors
    D. strong sanctions
11.___

12. Meticulous care must be exercised in writing the methodology section of the research report so that
    A. another investigator will achieve the same results if he repeats the study
    B. the interpretation of the findings cannot be challenged
    C. the report will be well balanced
    D. the rules of scientific logic are clearly indicated
12.___

13. When data are grouped into a frequency distribution, the   13.___
    true mode by definition is the _____ in the distribution
    A. 50% point
    B. largest single range
    C. point of greatest concentration
    D. smallest single range

14. Which of the following is LEAST likely to be a potential   14.___
    benefit arising from the use of electronic data process-
    ing systems?
    A. Analysis of more data and analysis of data in greater
       depth than manual systems
    B. Increased speed and accuracy in information processing
    C. Lower capital expenditures for office equipment
    D. Reduced personnel costs in tabulating and reporting
       functions

15. A *grapevine* is BEST defined as   15.___
    A. a harmful method of communication
    B. a system of communication operative below the
       executive level
    C. an informal communication system of no functional
       importance to an organization
    D. the internal and non-systematic channel of communi-
       cation within an organization

16. Of the following, the symbol shown at the   16.___
    right, as used in a systems flow chart, means
    A. document
    B. manual operation
    C. planning
    D. process

17. The mean age of a sample group drawn from population X is   17.___
    37.5 years and the standard error of the mean is 5.9.
    There is a 99% probability that the computed mean age of
    other samples drawn from population X would fall within
    the range of
    A. 31.6 - 43.4   B. 26.0 - 52.7
    C. 22.2 - 52.8   D. 20.0 - 55.0

18. After a budget has been developed, it serves to   18.___
    A. assist the accounting department in posting expendi-
       tures
    B. measure the effectiveness of department managers
    C. provide a yardstick against which actual costs are
       measured
    D. provide the operating department with total expen-
       ditures to date

19. In order to insure that work measurement or time study   19.___
    results will be consistent from one study to another,
    and reflect a fair day's work, the performance of the
    clerks must be rated or levelled.

Which of the following is LEAST likely to be included among the techniques for determining the performance level or for rating the study?
- A. Predetermined times
- B. Published rating tables
- C. Sampling studies
- D. Training films

20. Of the following, the BEST practice to follow when training a new employee is to
- A. encourage him to feel free to ask questions at any time
- B. immediately demonstrate how fast his job can be done so he will know what is expected of him
- C. let him watch other employees for a week or two
- D. point out mistakes after completion so he will learn by experience

20.___

21. An IMPORTANT aspect to keep in mind during the decision-making process is that
- A. all possible alternatives for attaining goals should be sought out and considered
- B. considering various alternatives only leads to confusion
- C. once a decision has been made, it cannot be retracted
- D. there is only one correct method to reach any goal

21.___

22. Implementation of accountability REQUIRES
- A. a leader who will not hesitate to take punitive action
- B. an established system of communication from the bottom to the top
- C. explicit directives from leaders
- D. too much expense to justify it

22.___

23. Of the following, the MAJOR difference between systems and procedures analysis and work simplification is:
- A. The former complicates organizational routine and the latter simplifies it
- B. The former is objective and the latter is subjective
- C. The former generally utilizes expert advice and the latter is a *do-it-yourself* improvement by supervisors and workers
- D. There is no difference other than in name

23.___

24. Systems development is concerned with providing
- A. a specific set of work procedures
- B. an overall framework to describe general relationships
- C. definitions of particular organizational functions
- D. organizational symbolism

24.___

25. Organizational systems and procedures should be
- A. developed as problems arise as no design can anticipate adequately the requirements of an organization
- B. developed jointly by experts in systems and procedures and the people who are responsible for implementing them

25.___

C. developed solely by experts in systems and procedures
D. eliminated whenever possible to save unnecessary expense

26. The CHIEF danger of a decentralized control system is that   26. B
    A. excessive reports and communications will be generated
    B. problem areas may not be detected readily
    C. the expense will become prohibitive
    D. this will result in too many *chiefs*

27. Of the following, management guides and controls clerical   27. D
    work PRINCIPALLY through
    A. close supervision and constant checking of personnel
    B. spot checking of clerical procedures
    C. strong sanctions for clerical supervisors
    D. the use of printed forms

28. Which of the following is MOST important before conduct-   28. C
    ing fact-finding interviews?
    A. Becoming acquainted with all personnel to be inter-
       viewed
    B. Explaining the techniques you plan to use
    C. Explaining to the operating officials the purpose
       and scope of the study
    D. Orientation of the physical layout

29. Of the following, the one that is NOT essential in carry-   29. B
    ing out a comprehensive work improvement program is
    A. standards of performance
    B. supervisory training
    C. work count/task list
    D. work distribution chart

30. Which of the following control techniques is MOST useful   30. D
    on large, complex systems projects?
    A. A general work plan   B. Gantt chart
    C. Monthly progress report   D. PERT chart

31. The action which is MOST effective in gaining acceptance   31. C
    of a study by the agency which is being studied is
    A. a directive from the agency head to install a study
       based on recommendations included in a report
    B. a lecture-type presentation following approval of
       the procedures
    C. a written procedure in narrative form covering the
       proposed system with visual presentations and dis-
       cussions
    D. procedural charts showing the *before* situation,
       forms, steps, etc. to the employees affected

32. Which of the following is NOT an advantage in the use of oral instructions as compared with written instructions? Oral instruction(s)
    A. can easily be changed
    B. is superior in transmitting complex directives
    C. facilitate exchange of information between a superior and his subordinate
    D. with discussions make it easier to ascertain understanding

32.___

33. Which organization principle is MOST closely related to procedural analysis and improvement?
    A. Duplication, overlapping, and conflict should be eliminated.
    B. Managerial authority should be clearly defined.
    C. The objectives of the organization should be clearly defined.
    D. Top management should be freed of burdensome detail.

33.___

34. Which one of the following is the MAJOR objective of operational audits?
    A. Detecting fraud
    B. Determining organization problems
    C. Determining the number of personnel needed
    D. Recommending opportunities for improving operating and management practices

34.___

35. Of the following, the formalization of organization structure is BEST achieved by
    A. a narrative description of the plan of organization
    B. functional charts
    C. job descriptions together with organization charts
    D. multi-flow charts

35.___

36. Budget planning is MOST useful when it achieves
    A. cost control   B. forecast of receipts
    C. performance review   D. personnel reduction

36.___

37. The UNDERLYING principle of sound administration is to
    A. base administration on investigation of facts
    B. have plenty of resources available
    C. hire a strong administrator
    D. establish a broad policy

37.___

37. Although questionnaires are not the best survey tool the management analyst has to use, there are times when a good questionnaire can expedite the *fact-finding* phase of a management survey.
Which of the following should be AVOIDED in the design and distribution of the questionnaire?
    A. Questions should be framed so that answers can be classified and tabulated for analysis.
    B. Those receiving the questionnaire must be knowledgeable enough to accurately provide the information desired.

37.___

(C) The questionnaire should enable the respondent to answer in a narrative manner.
   D. The questionnaire should require a minimum amount of writing.

39. Of the following, the formula which is used to calculate   39.___
    the arithmetic mean from data grouped in a frequency
    distribution is:
    M =

    A. $\dfrac{N}{\Sigma fX}$ B. $N(\Sigma fX)$ (C) $\dfrac{\Sigma fX}{N}$ D. $\dfrac{\Sigma X}{fN}$

40. Arranging large groups of numbers in frequency distribu-   40.___
    tions
    (A) gives a more composite picture of the total group
       than a random listing
    B. is misleading in most cases
    C. is unnecessary in most instances
    D. presents the data in a form whereby further manipu-
       lation of the group is eliminated

———

KEY (CORRECT ANSWERS)

1. B	11. A	21. A	31. C
2. C	12. A	22. B	32. B
3. D	13. C	23. C	33. A
4. A	14. C	24. B	34. D
5. C	15. D	25. B	35. C
6. C	16. B	26. B	36. A
7. A	17. C	27. D	37. A
8. B	18. C	28. C	38. C
9. A	19. C	29. B	39. C
10. A	20. A	30. D	40. A

———

EXAMINATION SECTION

TEST 1

DIRECTIONS: Each question or incomplete statement is followed by several suggested answers or completions. Select the one that BEST answers the question or completes the statement. *PRINT THE LETTER OF THE CORRECT ANSWER IN THE SPACE AT THE RIGHT.*

1. In performing a systems study, the analyst may find it necessary to prepare an accurate record of working statistics from departmental forms, questionnaires, and information gleaned in interviews.
   Which one of the following statements dealing with the statistical part of the study is the MOST valid?
   A. The emphasis of every survey is data collection.
   B. Data should not be represented in narrative form.
   C. The statistical report should include the titles of personnel required for each processing task.
   D. In gathering facts, the objective of a systems study should be the primary consideration.

1. D

2. The most direct method of obtaining information about activities in the area under study is by observation. There are several general rules for an analyst that are essential for observing and being accepted as an observer.
   The one of the following statements relating to this aspect of an analyst's responsibility that is most valid in the initial phase is that the analyst should NOT
   A. limit himself to observing only; he may criticize operations and methods
   B. prepare himself for what he is about to observe
   C. obtain permission of the department's management to actually perform some of the clerical tasks himself
   D. offer views of impending charges regarding new staff requirements, equipment, or procedures

2. D

3. The active concern of the systems analyst is the study and documentation of what he observes as it exists. Before attempting the actual study and documentation, the analyst should comply with certain generally accepted procedures.
   Of the following, the step the analyst should *generally* take FIRST is to
   A. define the problem and prepare a statement of objectives
   B. confer with the project director concerning persons to be interviewed
   C. accumulate data from all available sources within the area under study
   D. meet with operations managers to enlist their cooperation

3. A

4. During the course of any systems study, the analyst will have to gather some statistics if the operation model is to be realistic and meaningful.

4. B

With respect to the statistical report part of the study,
it is MOST valid to say that
- A. it must follow a standard format since there should
be no variation from one study to the next
- B. the primary factor to be considered is the volume of
work in the departmental unit at each stage of completion
- C. only variations that occur during peak and slow periods
should be recorded
- D. unless deadlines in the departmental units studied by
the analyst occur constantly, they should not be
taken into account

5. In systems analysis, the interview is one of the analyst's   5.___
major sources of information. In conducting an interview,
he should strive for immediate rapport with the operations
manager or department head with whom he deals.
With respect to his responsibility in this area, it is
considered LEAST appropriate for the analyst to
- A. explain the full background of the study and the
scope of the investigation
- B. emphasize the importance of achieving the stated
objectives and review the plan of the project
- C. assume that the attitudes of the workers are less
important than those of the executives
- D. request the manager's assistance in the form of
questions, suggestions, and general cooperation

6. Large, complex endeavors often take a long time to implement. 6.___
The following statements relate to long lead times imposed
by large-scale endeavors.
Select the one usually considered to be LEAST valid.
- A. Where there are external sponsors who provide funds or
political support, they should be provided with some
demonstration of what is being accomplished.
- B. Long lead times simplify planning and diminish the
threat of obsolescence by assuring that objectives
will be updated by the time the project is nearing
completion.
- C. During the period when no tangible results are forthcoming, techniques must be found to assess progress.
- D. Employees, particularly scientific personnel, should
feel a sense of accomplishment or they may shy away
from research which involves long-term commitments.

7. In traditional management theory, administrators are   7.___
expected to collect and weigh facts and probabilities, make
an optimal decision and see that it is carried out.
In the management of large-scale development projects, such
a clear sequence of action is *generally* NOT possible
because of
- A. their limited duration
- B. the static and fixed balance of power among interest
groups
- C. continuous suppression of new *facts*
- D. constantly changing constraints and pressures

Questions 8-10.

DIRECTIONS: One of the most valuable parts of the systems package is the systems flowchart, a technique that aids. understanding of the work flow. A flowchart should depict all the intricacies of the work flow from start to finish in order to give the onlooker a solid picture at a glance. The table below contains symbols used by the analyst in flowcharting. In answering Questions 8 through 10, refer to the following figures.

Figure I

Figure II

Figure III

Figure IV

Figure V

Figure VI

Figure VII

Figure VIII

Figure IX

Figure X

Figure XI

Figure XII

Figure XIII

8. The symbol that is COMMONLY used to specify clerical procedures which are not essential to the main processing function and yet are part of the overall procedure is represented by Figure

    A. III   B. VI   C. XII   D. XIII

8._D_

9. An analyst wishes to designate the following activities: *File reports*; *Calculate average*; *Attach labels*. The MOST APPROPRIATE symbol to use is represented by Figure

    A. V   B. VI   C. VII   D. II

9._A_

10. A *Report*, *Journal*, or *Record* should be represented by Figure

    A. I   B. III   C. IX   D. XI

10._B_

Question 11.

DIRECTIONS: The following figures are often used in program and systems flowcharting.

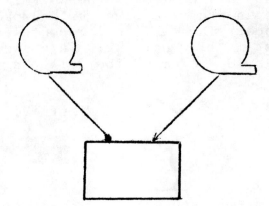

11. The above figures represent   11.___
     A. two magnetic tapes incorporated in a processing function
     B. two report   papers to be put in a cabinet in
        chronological order
     C. two transmittal tapes - both externally generated -
        routed to a vault
     D. an auxiliary operation involving two sequential decisions

12. When research and analysis of government programs, e.g.,   12.___
     pest control, drug rehabilitation, etc., is sponsored and
     conducted within a government unit, the scope of the analysis
     should *generally* be ____ the scope of the authority of the
     manager to whom the analyst is responsible.
     A. less than   B. less than or equal to
     C. greater than or equal to D. greater than

13. In recent years, there has been an increasing emphasis on   13.___
     outputs - the goods and services that a program produces.
     This emphasis on outputs imposes an information requirement.
     The one of the following which would MOST likely NOT be
     considered output information in a hospital or health care
     program is the
     A. number of patients cared for
     B. number of days patients were hospitalized
     C. budgeted monies for hospital beds
     D. quality of the service

14. Which one of the following statements pertaining to manage-   14.___
     ment information systems is generally considered to be
     LEAST valid?
     A. A management information system is a network of related
        subsystems developed according to an integrated scheme
        for evaluating the activities of an agency.
     B. A management information system specifies the content
        and format, the preparation and integration of informa-
        tion for all various functions within an agency that
        will best satisfy needs at various levels of management.

C. To operate a successful management information system, an agency will require a complex electronic computer installation.
D. The five elements which compose a management information system are: data input, files, data processing, procedures, and data output.

15. In the field of records management, electronic equipment is being used to handle office paperwork or data processing. With respect to such use, of the following, it is MOST valid to say that   15.____
    A. electronic equipment is not making great strides in the achievement of speed and economy in office paperwork
    B. electronic equipment accelerates the rate at which office paperwork is completed
    C. paperwork problems can be completely solved through mechanization
    D. introduction of electronic data processing equipment cuts down on the paper consumed in office processes

16. A reports control program evaluates the reporting requirements of top management so that reviews can be made of the existing reporting system to determine its adequacy.
Of the following statements pertaining to reports control, which is the MOST likely to be characteristic of such a program?   16.____
    A. Only the *exception* will be reported.
    B. Preparation of daily reports will be promoted.
    C. Executives will not delegate responsibility for preparing reports.
    D. Normal conditions are reported.

17. Which of the following types of work measurement techniques requires the HIGHEST degree of training and skill of technicians and supervisors and is MOST likely to involve the HIGHEST original cost?   17.____
    A. Work sampling
    B. Predetermined time standards
    C. The time study (stopwatch timing)
    D. Employee reporting

18. Which of the following types of work measurement techniques *generally* requires the LEAST amount of time to measure and establish standards?   18.____
    A. Work sampling
    B. Predetermined time standards
    C. The time study (stopwatch timing)
    D. Employee reporting

19. Assume that you, as an analyst, have been assigned to formally organize small work groups within a city department to perform a special project. After studying the project, you find you must choose between two possible approaches - either task teams or highly functionalized groups.   19.____

What would be one of the advantages of choosing the task-team approach over the highly functionalized organization?
  A. Detailed, centralized planning would be encouraged.
  B. Indifference to city goals and restrictions on output would be lessened.
  C. Work would be divided into very specialized areas.
  D. Superiors would be primarily concerned with seeing that subordinates do not deviate from the project.

20. In computer systems, which of the following direct-access file storage media has been found to be the MOST useful in real-time situations where the response time is *critical*?   20.___
  A. Disk   B. Drum
  C. Film strip   D. Magnetic card

KEY (CORRECT ANSWERS)

1. D		11. A	
2. D		12. B	
3. A		13. C	
4. B		14. C	
5. C		15. B	
6. B		16. A	
7. D		17. B	
8. D		18. A	
9. A		19. B	
10. B		20. B	

TEST 2

DIRECTIONS: Each question or incomplete statement is followed by several suggested answers or completions. Select the one that BEST answers the question or completes the statement. *PRINT THE LETTER OF THE CORRECT ANSWER IN THE SPACE AT THE RIGHT.*

1. Which one of the following types of computer program storage media is MOST appropriate in a situation in which the ability to make immediate program corrections and last-minute program changes is necessary?   1. D
   A. Magnetic tape   B. Disk
   C. Drum   D. Card

2. Which of the following statements is MOST appropriate to batch processing, as opposed to direct access processing, in the handling of file data?   It   2. C
   A. permits the master file to be kept in sequential order or stored at random
   B. permits a single file record to be read and processed immediately
   C. permits virtually unlimited amounts of data storage
   D. is a comparatively expensive method

3. The one of the following computer languages which is the MOST WIDELY used for business purposes is   3. D
   A. FORTRAN   B. PL/1   C. ALGOL   D. COBOL

4. Assume that an analyst is preparing an analysis of a departmental program. His investigation leads him to a potential problem relating to the program. The analyst thinks the potential problem is so serious that he cannot rely on preventive actions to remove the cause or significantly reduce the probability of its occurrence.   4. C
   Of the following, the MOST appropriate way for the analyst to promptly handle this serious matter described above would be to
   A. apply systematic afterthought to the achievement of objectives by analysis of the problem
   B. compare actual performance with the expected standard of performance
   C. prepare contingency actions to be adopted immediately if the problem does occur
   D. identify, locate, and describe the deviation from the standard

5. Assume that an analyst is directed to investigate a problem relating to organizational behavior in his agency and to prepare a report thereon. After reviewing the preliminary draft, his superior cautions him to overcome his tendency to misuse and overgeneralize his interpretation of existing knowledge.   5. ___

Which one of the following statements appearing in the
draft is MOST *usually* considered to be a common distortion
of behavioral science knowledge?
 (A) Pay -- even incentive pay -- isn't very important
     anymore.
 B. There are nonrational aspects to people's behavior.
 C. The informal system exerts much control over organi-
    zational participants.
 D. Employees have many motives.

Questions 6-10.

DIRECTIONS: Each of Questions 6 through 10 consists of a statement
             which contains one word that is incorrectly used because
             it is not in keeping with the meaning that the quotation
             is evidently intended to convey. Determine which word
             is incorrectly used. Then select from the words lettered
             A, B, C, or D the word which, when substituted for the
             incorrectly used word, would BEST help to convey the
             meaning of the statement.

6.   While the utilization of cost-benefit analysis in decision-   6.___
     making processes should be encouraged, it must be well under-
     stood that there are many limitations on the constraints of
     the analysis. One must be cautioned against using cost-
     benefit procedures automatically and blindly. Still, society
     will almost certainly be better off with the application of
     cost-benefit methods than it would be without them. As some
     authorities aptly point out, an important advantage of a cost-
     benefit study is that it forces those responsible to quantify
     costs and benefits as far as possible rather than rest content
     with vague qualitative judgments or personal hunches. Also,
     such an analysis has the very valuable by-product of causing
     questions to be asked which would otherwise not have been
     raised. Finally, even if cost-benefit analysis cannot give
     the right answer, it can sometimes play the purely negative
     role of screening projects and rejecting those answers which
     are obviously less promising.
        A. precise   B. externally
        (C) applicability   D. unresponsiveness

7.   The programming method used by the government should attempt 7.___
     to assess the costs and benefits of individual projects, in
     comparison with private and other public alternatives. The
     program, then, consists of the most meritorious projects
     that the budget will design. Meritorious projects excluded
     from the budget provide arguments for increasing its size.
     There are difficulties inherent in the specific project
     approach. The attempt is to apply profit criteria in public
     projects analogous to those used in evaluating private
     projects. This involves comparison of monetary values of
     present and future costs and benefits. But, in many important
     cases, such as highways, parkways, and bridges, the product
     of the government's investment does not directly enter the
     market economy. Consequently, evaluation requires imputation
     of market values. For example, the returns on a bridge have

been estimated by attempting to value the time saved by users. Such measurements necessarily contain a strong element of artificiality.
   A. annulled   B. expedient   C. accommodate D. marginally

8. Consider the problem of budgeting for activities designed   8.___
    to alleviate poverty and rooted unemployment. Are skill retraining efforts better or worse investments than public works? Are they better or worse than subsidies or other special incentives to attract new industry? Or, at an even more fundamental level, is a dollar invested in an attempt to rehabilitate a mature, technologically displaced, educationally handicapped, unemployed man a better commitment than a comparable dollar invested in supporting the educational and technical preparation of his son for employment in a different line of work? The questions may look unreasonable, even unanswerable. But the fact is that they are implicitly answered in any budget decision in the defined problem area. The only subordinate issue is whether the answer rests on intuition and guess, or on a budget system that presents relevant information so organized as to contribute to rational analysis, planning, and decision-making.
    A. incomplete   B. relevant
    C. significant   D. speculate

9. Choices among health programs, on the basis of cost-benefit   9.___
    analysis, raise another set of ethical problems. Measuring discounted lifetime earnings does not reveal the value of alleviating pain and suffering; some diseases have a high death rate, others are debilitating, others are merely uncomfortable. In general, choices among health and education programs that are predicated on discounted lifetime earnings will structure the choice against those who have low earnings, those whose earnings will materialize only at some future point in time, or those whose participation in the labor force is limited. It may be an appropriate economic policy to reduce expenditures in areas that maximize the future level of national income. But the maximization of social welfare may dictate attention to considerations, such as equality of opportunity, that transcend the limitations of values defined in such narrow terms.
    A. concentrate B. divergent C. enforcing   D. favorably

10. Without defined and time-phased objectives, it is difficult 10.___
    to be critical of administrative performance. To level a charge of waste or malperformance at the managers of a public program is, of course, one of the more popular pastimes of any administration's loyal opposition. But it is a rare experience to find such a charge documented by the kind of precise cost-effectiveness measures that are the common test of the quality of management performance in a well-run organization. Those who take a professional view of management responsibility are even more concerned about the acceptance of the kind of information that would enable a manager to assess the progress and quality of his own

performance and, as appropriate, to initiate corrective
action before outside criticism can even start.
    A. absence   B. rebut   C. withdraw   D. impeded

11. What is the relationship between the cost of inputs and
the value of outputs when the results obtained from a
program can be measured in money? _____ ratio.
    A. Value administrative-cost B. Break-even point
    C. Variable-direct   D. Cost-benefit

11. D

12. Some writers in the field of public expenditure have noted
a disturbing tendency inherent in cost-benefit analysis.
Which one of the following statements MOST accurately
expresses their concern over the use of cost-benefit analysis? It
    A. encourages the attachment of monetary values to
       intangibles
    B. has a built-in neglect of measurable outcomes while
       emphasizing the nonmeasurable
    C. consciously exaggerates social values and overstates
       political values
    D. encourages emphasis of those costs and benefits that
       cannot be measured rather than those that can

12. A

13. In private industry, budgetary control begins logically
with an estimate of sales and the income therefrom.
Of the following, the term used in government which is
MOST analogous to that of sales in private industry is
    A. borrowed funds   B. the amount appropriated
    C. general overhead   D. surplus funds

13. B

14. When constructing graphs of causally related variables,
how should the variables be placed to conform to conventional use?
    A. The independent variable should be placed on the
       vertical axis and the dependent variable on the
       horizontal axis.
    B. The dependent variable should be placed on the
       vertical axis and the independent variable on the
       horizontal axis.
    C. Independent variables should be placed on both axes.
    D. Dependent variables should be placed on both axes.

14. B

Questions 15-18.

DIRECTIONS: Answer Questions 15 through 18 on the basis of the
                 following graph describing the output of keypunch
                 operators.

Number of cards
punched per hour
(based on 20 items
punched per card)

time

15. Of the following, during what four-year period did the   15. A
    AVERAGE OUTPUT of keypunch operators *fall below* 100 cards
    per hour?
        A. 1977-80   B. 1978-81   C. 1980-83   D. 1981-84

16. The AVERAGE PERCENTAGE CHANGE in output over the previous   16. B
    year's output for the years 1979 to 1982 is MOST NEARLY
        A. 2   B. 0   C. -5   D. -7

17. The DIFFERENCE between the actual output for 1982 and the   17. C
    projected figure based upon the average increase from
    1976 to 1981 is MOST NEARLY
        A. 18   B. 20   C. 22   D. 24

18. Assume that after constructing the above graph, you, an   18. C
    analyst, discovered that the average number of items punched
    per card in 1982 was 25 (instead of 20) because of the com-
    plex nature of the work performed during that period.
    The AVERAGE OUTPUT in cards per hour for the period 1980 to
    1983, expressed in terms of 20 items per card, would then
    be APPROXIMATELY
        A. 95   B. 100   C. 105   D. 110

19. Assume that Unit S's production fluctuated substantially   19. B
    from one year to another. In 1979, Unit S's production
    was 100% greater than in 1978; in 1980, it was 25% less
    than in 1979; and in 1981, it was 10% greater than in 1980.
    On the basis of this information, it is CORRECT to conclude
    that Unit S's production in 1981 exceeded its production
    in 1978 by
        A. 50%   B. 65%   C. 75%   D. 90%

20. Statistical sampling is often used in administrative   20. ____
operations primarily because it enables
   A. administrators to make staff selections
   B. decisions to be made based on mathematical and
      scientific fact
   C. courses of action to be determined by electronic
      data processing or computer programs
   D. useful predictions to be made from relatively small
      samples

KEY (CORRECT ANSWERS)

1.	D	11.	D
2.	C	12.	A
3.	D	13.	B
4.	C	14.	B
5.	A	15.	A
6.	C	16.	B
7.	C	17.	C
8.	C	18.	C
9.	A	19.	B
10.	A	20.	D

EXAMINATION SECTION
TEST 1

DIRECTIONS: Each question or incomplete statement is followed by
several suggested answers or completions. Select the
one that BEST answers the question or completes the
statement. *PRINT THE LETTER OF THE CORRECT ANSWER IN
THE SPACE AT THE RIGHT.*

1. Of the following, the BEST statement concerning the place-   1. C
ment of *Conclusions and Recommendations* in a management
report is:
   A. Recommendations should always be included in a report
      unless the report presents the results of an investiga-
      tion
   B. If a report presents conclusions, it must present
      recommendations
   C. Every statement that is a conclusion should grow out of
      facts given elsewhere in the report
   D. Conclusions and recommendations should always conclude
      the report because they depend on its contents

2. Assume you are preparing a systematic analysis of your   2. B
agency's pest control program and its effect on eliminating
rodent infestation of premises in a specific region.
To omit from your report important facts which you originally
received from the person to whom you are reporting is
GENERALLY considered to be
   A. *desirable*; anyone who is likely to read the report can
      consult his files for extra information
   B. *undesirable*; the report should include major facts
      that are obtained as a result of your efforts
   C. *desirable*; the person you are reporting to does not
      pass the report on to others who lack his own familiarity
      with the subject
   D. *undesirable*; the report should include all of the
      facts that are obtained as a result of your efforts

3. Of all the nonverbal devices used in report writing,   3. B
tables are used most frequently to enable a reader to
compare statistical information more easily. Hence, it
is important that an analyst know when to use tables.
Which one of the following statements that relate to tables
is generally considered to be LEAST valid?
   A. A table from an outside source must be acknowledged
      by the report writer.
   B. A table should be placed far in advance of the point
      where it is referred to or discussed in the report.
   C. The notes applying to a table are placed at the bottom
      of the table, rather than at the bottom of the page
      on which the table is found.
   D. A table should indicate the major factors that effect
      the data it contains.

4. Assume that an analyst writes reports which contain more detail than might be needed to serve their purpose. Such a practice is GENERALLY considered to be
   A. *desirable*; this additional detail permits maximized machine utilization
   B. *undesirable*; if specifications of reports are defined when they are first set up, loss of flexibility will follow
   C. *desirable*; everything ought to be recorded so it will be there if it is ever needed
   D. *undesirable*; recipients of these reports are likely to discredit them entirely

5. Assume that an analyst is gathering certain types of information which can be obtained only through interrogation of the clientele by means of a questionnaire. Which one of the following statements that relate to construction of the questionnaire is the MOST valid?
   A. Stress, whenever possible, the use of leading questions.
   B. Avoid questions which touch on personal prejudice or pride.
   C. Opinions, as much as facts, should be sought.
   D. There is no psychological advantage for starting with a question of high interest value.

Questions 6-10.

DIRECTIONS: Questions 6 through 10 consist of sentences lettered A, B, C, and D. For each question, choose the sentence which is stylistically and grammatically MOST appropriate for a management report.

6. A. For too long, the citizen has been forced to rely for his productivity information on the whims, impressions and uninformed opinion of public spokesmen.
   B. For too long, the citizen has been forced to base his information about productivity on the whims, impressions and uninformed opinion of public spokesmen.
   C. The citizen has been forced to base his information about productivity on the whims, impressions and uninformed opinion of public spokesmen for too long.
   D. The citizen has been forced for too long to rely for his productivity information on the whims, impressions and uninformed opinion of public spokesmen.

7. A. More competition means lower costs to the city, thereby helping to compensate for inflation.
   B. More competition, helping to compensate for inflation, means lower costs to the city.
   C. Inflation may be compensated for by more competition, which will reduce the city's costs.
   D. The costs to the city will be lessened by more competition, helping to compensate for inflation.

8. A. Some objectives depend on equal efforts from others, particularly private interests and the federal government; for example, technical advancement.
    B. Some objectives, such as technical advancement, depend on equal efforts from others, particularly private interests and the federal government.
    C. Some objectives depend on equal efforts from others, particularly private interests and the federal government, such as technical advancement.
    D. Some objectives depend on equal efforts from others (technical advancement, for example); particularly private interests and the federal government.

 8. B

9. A. It has always been the practice of this office to effectuate recruitment of prospective employees from other departments.
    B. This office has always made a practice of recruiting prospective employees from other departments.
    C. Recruitment of prospective employees from other departments has always been a practice which has been implemented by this office.
    D. Implementation of the policy of recruitment of prospective employees from other departments has always been a practice of this office.

9. B

10. A. These employees are assigned to the level of work evidenced by their efforts and skills during the training period.
    B. The level of work to which these employees is assigned is decided upon on the basis of the efforts and skills evidenced by them during the period in which they were trained.
    C. Assignment of these employees is made on the basis of the level of work their efforts and skills during the training period has evidenced.
    D. These employees are assigned to a level of work their efforts and skills during the training period have evidenced.

 10. A

11. To overcome the manual collation problem, forms are frequently padded.
    Of the following statements which relate to this type of packaging, select the one that is MOST accurate.
    A. Typewritten forms which are prepared as padded forms are more efficient than all other packaging.
    B. Padded forms are best suited for handwritten forms.
    C. It is difficult for a printer to pad form copies of different colors.
    D. Registration problems increase when cut-sheet forms are padded.

11. ___

12. Most forms are cut from a standard mill sheet of paper. 12.C
This is the size on which forms dealers base their prices.
Since an agency is paying for a full-size sheet of paper,
it is the responsibility of the analyst to design forms
so that as many as possible may be cut from the sheet
without waste.
Of the following sizes, select the one that will cut from
a standard mill sheet with the GREATEST waste and should,
therefore, be avoided if possible.
    A. 4" x 6"   B. 5" x 8"   C. 9" x 12"   D. 8½" x 14"

13. Assume that you are assigned the task of reducing the time 13.B
and costs involved in completing a form that is frequently
used in your agency. After analyzing the matter, you
decide to reduce the writing requirements of the form
through the use of ballot boxes and preprinted data.
If exact copy-to-copy registration of this form is
necessary, it is MOST advisable to
    A. vary the sizes of the ballot boxes
    B. stagger the ballot boxes
    C. place the ballot boxes as close together as possible
    D. have the ballot boxes follow the captions

14. To overcome problems that are involved in the use of cut- 14.D
sheet and padded forms, specialty forms have been developed.
Normally, these forms are commercially manufactured rather
than produced in-plant. Before designing a form as a
specialty form, however, you should be assured that certain
factors are present.
Which one of the following factors deserves LEAST consideration?
    A. The form is to be used in quantities of 5,000 or more
       annually.
    B. The forms will be prepared on equipment using either
       a pinfeed device or pressure rollers for continuous
       feed-through.
    C. Two or more copies of the form set must be held
       together for further processing subsequent to the
       initial distribution of the form set.
    D. Copies of the form will be identical and no items of
       data will be selectively eliminated from one or more
       copies of the form.

15. Although a well-planned form should require little explana- 15.A
tion as to its completion, there are many occasions when
the analyst will find it necessary to include instructions
on the form to assure that the person completing it does
so correctly.
With respect to such instructions, it is usually considered
to be LEAST appropriate to place them
    A. in footnotes at the bottom of the form
    B. following the spaces to be completed
    C. directly under the form's title
    D. on the front of the form

16. One of the basic data-arrangement methods used in forms   16. B
    design is the *on-line* method. When this method is used,
    captions appear on the same line as the space provided
    for entry of the variable data.
    This arrangement is NOT recommended because it
       A. forces the typist to make use of the typewriter's
          tab stops, thus increasing processing time
       B. wastes horizontal space since the caption appears
          on the writing line
       C. tends to make the variable data become more dominant
          than the captions
       D. increases the form's processing time by requiring the
          typist to continually roll the platen back and forth
          to expose the caption

17. Before designing a form for his agency, the analyst   17. C
    should be aware of certain basic design standards.
    Which one of the following statements relating to horizon-
    tal and vertical spacing requirements is *generally*
    considered to be the MOST acceptable in forms design?
       A. If the form will be completed by typewriter, no more
          than four writing lines to the vertical inch should
          be allowed.
       B. If the form will be completed by hand, allowance
          should not be made for the different sizes of
          individual handwriting.
       C. If the form will be completed partly by hand and
          partly by typewriter, the analyst should provide
          the same vertical spacing as for typewriter completion.
       D. The form should be designed with proportional spacing
          for pica and elite type.

18. As an analyst, you may be required to conduct a functional   18. C
    analysis of your agency's forms.
    Which one of the following statements pertaining to this
    type of analysis is *generally* considered to be MOST valid?
       A. Except for extremely low-volume forms, all forms
          should be functionally analyzed.
       B. To obtain maximum benefit from the analysis, func-
          tional re-analyses of all forms should be undertaken
          at least once every three to six months.
       C. All existing forms should be functionally analyzed
          before reorder.
       D. Only new forms should be functionally analyzed prior
          to being authorized for adoption.

19. The analyst must assure the users of a form that its   19. A
    construction provides for the most efficient method in
    terms of how data will be entered and processed subsequent
    to their initial entry.
    While the simplest construction is the cut sheet, the
    GREATEST disadvantage of this type of construction is
       A. the non-productive *makeready* time required if multiple
          copies of a form must be simultaneously prepared
       B. the difficulty experienced by users in filling in the
          forms solely by mechanical means

C. its uneconomical cost of production
D. the restrictions of limitations placed on the utilization of a variety of substances which may be used in form composition

20. Assume you have designed a form which requires data to be entered on multiple copies simultaneously. A determination has not yet been made whether to order the form as interleaved-carbon form sets or as carbonless forms. The advantage of using carbonless forms is that they
    A. permit more readable copies to be made at a single writing
    B. average about 30 percent lower in price than conventional interleaved-carbon form sets
    C. provide greater security if the information entered on the form is classified
    D. are not subject to accidental imaging

20. C

KEY (CORRECT ANSWERS)

1. C		11. B
2. B		12. C
3. B		13. B
4. D		14. D
5. B		15. A
6. B		16. B
7. A		17. C
8. B		18. C
9. B		19. A
10. A		20. C

TEST 2

DIRECTIONS: Each question or incomplete statement is followed by several suggested answers or completions. Select the one that BEST answers the question or completes the statement. *PRINT THE LETTER OF THE CORRECT ANSWER IN THE SPACE AT THE RIGHT.*

1. Many analysts lean toward the use of varying colors of paper in a multiple-part form set to indicate distribution. This usage is GENERALLY considered to be
   A. *desirable*; it is more effective than using white paper for all copies and imprinting the distribution in the margin of the copy
   B. *undesirable*; colored inks should be used instead to indicate distribution in a multi-part form set
   C. *desirable*; it will lead to lower costs of form production
   D. *undesirable*; it causes operational difficulties if the form is to be microfilmed or optically scanned

1.

2. After a form has been reviewed and approved by the analyst, it should be given an identifying number. The following items pertain to the form number.
   Which item is MOST appropriately included as a portion of the form number?
   A. Revision date
   B. Order quantity
   C. Retention period
   D. Organization unit responsible for the form

2.

Questions 3-8.

DIRECTIONS: Questions 3 through 8 should be answered on the basis of the following information.

Assume that the figure at the top of the next page is a systems flowchart specifically prepared for the purchasing department of a large municipal agency. Some of the symbols in the flowchart are incorrectly used. The symbols are numbered.

3. According to the flowchart, Number 2 is
    A. *correct*
    B. *incorrect*; the symbol should have six sides
    C. *incorrect*; the symbol should be the same as Number 7
    D. *incorrect*; the symbol should be the same as Number 8

4. According to the flowchart, Number 9 is
    A. *correct*
    B. *incorrect*; the symbol should be the same as Number 1
    C. *incorrect*; the symbol should be the same as Number 7
    D. *incorrect*; the symbol should be the same as Number 10

5. According to the flowchart, Number 11 is   5. D
    A. *correct*
    B. *incorrect*; the symbol should be the same as Number 13
    C. *incorrect*; the symbol should be the same as Number 10
    (D) *incorrect*; the symbol should be the same as Number 9

6. According to the flowchart, Number 14 is   6. C
    A. *correct*
    B. *incorrect*; the symbol should have three sides
    (C) *incorrect*; the symbol should have six sides
    D. *incorrect*; the symbol should have eight sides

7. According to the flowchart, Number 12 is   7. A
    (A) *correct*
    B. *incorrect*; a *file* should be represented in the same
       form as the symbol which immediately precedes it
    C. *incorrect*; the symbol should be the same as Number 13
    D. *incorrect*; the symbol should be the same as Number 14

8. According to the flowchart, Number 15 is   8. C
    A. *correct*

    B. *incorrect*; the symbol should be

    (C) *incorrect*; the symbol should be

    D. *incorrect*; the symbol should be

9. An agency expects to increase its services, the workload   9. A
of the office will increase, and additional equipment and
personnel will probably be required. Although there is
no set formula for determining how much space will be
required in an agency in a specific number of years from
now, certain guidelines have been developed to assist the
analyst in dealing with the problem of providing expansion
space.
Which of the following statements pertaining to this aspect
of space utilization is *generally* considered to be the
LEAST desirable practice?
    (A) Spread the departments to fit into space that is
       temporarily surplus and awaiting the day when it is
       needed
    B. Place major departments where they can expand into
       the area of minor departments
    C. Visualize the direction in which the expansion will go
       and avoid placing the relatively fixed installations
       in the way
    D. Lay out the departments economically and screen off
       the surplus areas, using them for storage or other
       temporary usage

Questions 10-11.

DIRECTIONS: Questions 10 and 11 are based on the following layout.

Layout of Conference Room
BUREAU OF RODENT CONTROL

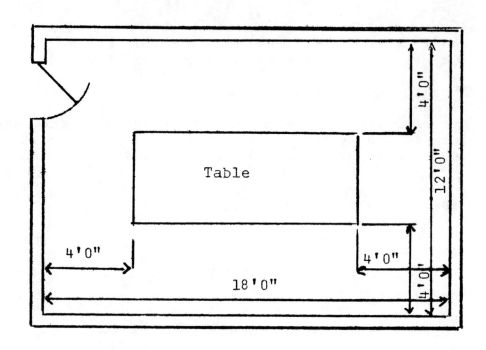

10. The LARGEST number of persons that can be accommodated   10.___
     in the area shown in the layout is
        A. 16   B. 10   C. 8   D. 6

11. Assume that the Bureau's programs undergo expansion and   11.___
     the Director indicates that the feasibility of increasing
     the size of the conference room should be explored.
     For every two additional persons that are to be accommodated,
     the analyst should recommend that ____ be added to table
     length and ____ be added to room length.
        A. 2'-6"; 2'-6"   B. 5'-0"; 5'-0"
        C. 2'-6"; 5'-0"   D. 5'-0"; 2'-6"

Questions 12-14.

DIRECTIONS: Questions 12 through 14 are based on the following
               information.

SYMBOLS USED IN LAYOUT WORK

Figure 1   ◯   Figure VIII

Figure II   ─◯   Figure IX

Figure III   ⊙   Figure X

Figure IV   ▣   Figure XI

Figure V   ─◯─   Figure XII

Figure VI   ◁

Figure VII   ▥

12. Figure XI is the symbol for   12.___
        A. a temporary partition   B. floor outlets
        C. ceiling outlets   D. a switch

13. A *solid post* is represented by Figure   13.___
        A. II   B. V   C. VIII   D. XII

14. Figure VI is the symbol for a(n)   14.___
        A. switch   B. intercom
        C. telephone outlet   D. railing

15. While there is no one office layout that will fit all   15.___
     organizations, there are some reasonably good principles
     of office layout by function that could be applied to any
     office situation.
     Which one of the following statements relating to functions
     and locations is MOST characteristic of a good layout?
     The
        A. personnel department is usually close to the reception
           area
        B. purchasing department should be far from the entrance
        C. data processing activity and duplicating services are
           normally placed together
        D. top management group is usually dispersed throughout
           the general office group

16. Records are valuable to an organization becaused recorded   16.___
     information is more accurate and enduring than oral informa-
     tion.
     Of the following, the MOST important stage in records
     management is at the
        A. storage stage
        B. time when quality control principles are applied
        C. point of distribution
        D. source when records are created

17. The rough layout of an office can be made by sketching   17.
the office floor plan from actual measurements, or it can
be copied from blueprints furnished by the building
management.
As an analyst assigned to improve an office layout, you
should be aware that the experienced layout man prefers
to make his sketch from
   A. a blueprint because it eliminates the extra work in
      checking a sketch made from it
   B. actual measurements because a blueprint is in a
      scale of $\frac{1}{4}$ or $\frac{1}{2}$ inch to a foot instead of the
      preferred 1/8 inch scale
   C. a blueprint because he can always trust the blueprint
   D. actual measurements because he has to sketch in the
      desks and other equipment

18. Planning the traffic flow and appropriate aisle space in   18.
an office are factors an analyst must consider in any
desk arrangement.
Of the following, it is *generally* the MOST desirable
practice to
   A. deny requests to rearrange desks to give employees
      more working space if the space left for the aisle
      is more than needed for the traffic
   B. figure operating space and the open file drawer
      separately from the allowance for the aisle if files
      must open into the aisle
   C. conserve space by making the main aisle in an office
      no wider than 36 inches
   D. disregard the length of feeders to an aisle in deter-
      mining the width of the aisle

19. Code systems which are used to mark records for long- or   19.
short-term retention are easy to devise and use.
Accordingly, of the following situations, it would be MOST
appropriate to use the *destroy code* for
   A. information that calls for action within 90 days and
      for which no record is necessary thereafter
   B. information that may be needed for evaluation of past
      agency activities
   C. records which contain information that is readily
      available elsewhere
   D. records that contain information necessary for audit
      requirements

20. Assume your agency is moving into new quarters and you   20.
will assist your superior in assigning space to the various
offices. The offices will be air-conditioned. The
interior of the space to be assigned is located away from
windows.
Of the following, it is MOST appropriate for you to recommend
that the interior of the space be set aside for
   A. legal offices and confidential investigation sections
   B. visitors to the agency
   C. conference and training rooms
   D. typing and stenographic pools

KEY (CORRECT ANSWERS)

1. D
2. A
3. A
4. B
5. D

6. C
7. A
8. C
9. A
10. B

11. A
12. A
13. D
14. C
15. A

16. D
17. D
18. B
19. C
20. C

EXAMINATION SECTION

TEST 1

DIRECTIONS: Each question or incomplete statement is followed by several suggested answers or completions. Select the one that BEST answers the question or completes the statement. *PRINT THE LETTER OF THE CORRECT ANSWER IN THE SPACE AT THE RIGHT.*

1. In organizational theory, the optimum span of control, that is, the number of subordinates who can be effectively supervised by one man above the level of the first line supervisor, is GENERALLY set at between
   A. 3 and 6   B. 6 and 12   C. 12 and 18   D. 18 and 24   1. A

2. Which of the following is LEAST desirable as a basic guide to normal conventional office layout?   2. C
   A. Arrange desks so that work flows in a normal fashion.
   B. Place files nearest to the persons who will use them.
   C. Utilize a number of small areas to provide privacy.
   D. Utilize one single large area.

3. *A set of objects together with relationships between the objects and between their attributes* is the definition of   3. A
   A. a perceptual whole and its subcomponents
   B. a system in the terms of specific systems theory
   C. an organism
   D. forms control

4. A technique of time study in which each employee maintains a record of his own time is GENERALLY known as _____ study.   4. C
   A. estimated time   B. observed time
   C. time log   D. wristwatch

5. An employee has approached a supervisor with a request for a change involving his personal status or with a suggestion for making an improvement in the work. The supervisor knows that the suggestion cannot be granted.   5. C
   Of the following, the BEST procedure would be for the supervisor to
   A. refer the matter to the personnel department
   B. refer the matter to his superior for action
   C. reject the proposal, explaining the defects or objections which cannot be overcome
   D. shelve the idea so that the employee will realize it cannot be acted upon

6. There are, in general, a number of common methods of drawing samples for statistical work.   6. C
   The method in which a regularly ordered interval is maintained between the items chosen is BEST termed _____ sampling.
   A. random   B. stratified or selective
   C. systematic   D. work

7. The multi-column process chart can be put to all of the
   following general uses EXCEPT to
   A. improve office layout   B. improve procedures
   C. standardize procedures   D. train personnel

   7. A

8. If one wished to show the percentage of change over a
   period of time, the MOST appropriate type of graph or
   chart GENERALLY would be the _____ chart.
   A. bar
   B. line or curve
   C. logarithmic or semi-logarithmic
   D. pie

   8. C

9. A chart designed for the explicit purpose of portraying
   graphically information relating to the degree of responsibility of key individuals for the performance of various
   functions is BEST described as a(n) _____ chart.
   A. linear responsibility   B. work distribution
   C. work process   D. staff

   9. A

10. The technique of work measurement LEAST useful for setting
    up a program of office incentive pay GENERALLY would be
    A. log sheets   B. stopwatch time study
    C. wristwatch time study   D. work sampling

    10. A

11. There are a number of steps to be taken in making a work
    sampling study in order to set production standards. Three
    of the steps listed below are peculiar only to work samp-
    ling, in contrast with other work measurement techniques.
    The one EXCEPTION is:
    A. Define the breakdown of work into the proper elements
       of work and no-work or delay to be observed
    B. Determine the required number of observations needed
       for the specified degree of reliability
    C. Establish the observation intervals
    D. Make a preliminary estimate of work and no-work or
       delay element percentages for step A

    11. A

12. A number of standardized flow process chart symbols have
    been generally accepted.
    The symbol $\bar{\nabla}$ GENERALLY indicates a(n)
    A. delay   B. storage or file
    C. inspection   D. operation

    12. B

13. A number of standardized flow process chart symbols have
    been generally accepted.
    The symbol [   ]   GENERALLY indicates a(n)
    A. delay   B. storage or file
    C. inspection   D. operation

    13. C

14. The type of work for which short interval scheduling
    generally would be LEAST applicable would be the work of
    a group of
    A. calculating clerks
    B. order clerks
    C. technically-oriented clerks
    D. typists

    14. C

15. In writing a business report, the BEST expression to use,   15. <u>A</u>
    in general, of those listed below would NORMALLY be:
    A. Because   B. Inasmuch as
    C. In view of the fact that D. With reference to

16. Of the following, the MAJOR advantage of a random access   16. <u>D</u>
    data processing system, as compared with a sequential-type
    system, is its
    A. ability to use more than one input system
    B. demand for more sophisticated systems and programming
    C. greater storage capacity and access speed
    D. potential for processing data on a *first-come, first-
       served* basis

17. A good rule to remember with regard to decision making   17. <u>B</u>
    is that decisions should be made
    A. at the highest level competent to make such a
       decision
    B. at the lowest level competent to make such a decision
    C. by the person responsible for carrying out the
       decision
    D. by the person responsible for the work of the unit

18. Which of the following potential systems would LEAST   18. <u>C</u>
    likely be improved by being on-line? A(n) _____ system.
    A. budgeting control   B. welfare eligibility
    C. employee payroll   D. inventory control

19. A management information and control system essentially   19. <u>A</u>
    should be designed to provide management personnel with
    up-to-date information which will enable them to improve
    control over their operations.
    In designing such a system, the FIRST step to determine
    is:
    A. What information is needed to effectively control
       operations?
    B. What information is presently available?
    C. What organization changes are necessary to implement
       the system?
    D. Who is presently processing the information that
       might be used?

20. In designing control reports, which of the following   20. <u>B</u>
    guidelines is of MOST importance?
    A. Financial information should always be carried to
       the nearest penny.
    B. The report should be a simple and concise statement
       of only the pertinent facts
    C. The report should indicate the source of original
       data and how the computations were made.
    D. The report should have the broadest possible dis-
       tribution at all levels of management.

21. A situation which enables a number of users at remote locations to have access to a SINGLE computer is called
    A. multiprocessing
    B. multiprogramming
    C. process overlap
    D. time sharing

21. D

22. The computer device which would offer the GREATEST speed in reading input is the
    A. CRT display
    B. magnetic tape
    C. optical scanner
    D. paper tape

22. A

23. Which of the following steps is LEAST desirable in designing an electronic data processing system?
    A. Design the EDP system first, then relate it to current operations.
    B. Develop a corollary chart for the corresponding flow of information
    C. Develop a flow chart for the functions affected by the system
    D. Obtain from available EDP equipment that which best fits current operations

23. A

24. Electronic data processing equipment can produce more information faster than can be generated by any other means. Because this is true, one wonders whether our ability to generate information has not far outstripped our ability to assimilate it.
    In view of this, a PERSISTENT danger management faces is in
    A. determining the budget for management information systems
    B. determining what information is of real worth
    C. finding enough computer personnel
    D. keeping their computers fully occupied

24. B

25. The one of the following that is an ADVANTAGE of a visual display terminal over the typewriter-type terminal employed in an on-line system is:
    A. Information retrieval is somewhat faster
    B. Operators can be trained more easily
    C. There is no advantage
    D. They are less expensive to operate

25. A

KEY (CORRECT ANSWERS)

1. A		11. A	
2. C		12. B	
3. A		13. C	
4. C		14. C	
5. C		15. A	
6. C		16. D	
7. A		17. B	
8. C		18. C	
9. A		19. A	
10. A		20. B	

21. D
22. A
23. A
24. B
25. A

TEST 2

DIRECTIONS: Each question or incomplete statement is followed by several suggested answers or completions. Select the one that BEST answers the question or completes the statement. *PRINT THE LETTER OF THE CORRECT ANSWER IN THE SPACE AT THE RIGHT.*

1. In analyzing data for the acquisition of new equipment, an analyst gathers the facts, analyzes them, and develops new procedures which will be required when the new equipment arrives.
   In analyzing the factors involved, which one of the following is normally LEAST important in the evaluation of new equipment?
   A. Cost factors
   B. Layout and installation factors
   C. Production planning
   D. Operational experience of manufacturers of allied equipment

   1. D

2. If an analyst is required to recommend the selection of a machine for an office operation, he can BEST judge the expected output of a particular machine by pursuing which of the following courses of action?
   Obtain
   A. an actual test run of the machine in his office
   B. data from the manufacturer of the machine
   C. information on the percentage of working time the machine will be used
   D. the experience of actual users of similar machines elsewhere

   2. A

3. Of the following, the BEST definition of records management is
   A. storage of all types of records at minimum expense
   B. planned control of all types of records
   C. storage of records for maximum accessibility
   D. systematic filing of all types of records

   3. B

4. The one of the following which is NOT a primary objective of a records retention and disposal system is to
   A. assure appropriate preservation of records having permanent value
   B. dispose of records not warranting further preservation
   C. establish retention standards for archives
   D. provide an opportunity to use miniaturization

   4. D

5. Of the following functions of management, the one which should NORMALLY precede the others is
   A. coordinating   B. directing
   C. organizing   D. planning

   5. D

6. One of the more famous studies of organizations is called   6.___
   the Hawthorne study.
   This work was one of the first to point out the importance
   of
       A. employee's benefit and retirement programs
       B. informal organization among employees
       C. job engineering
       D. styles of position classification

7. In organization theory, the type of position in which an   7.___
   individual is appointed to give technical aid to management on a particular problem area is generally BEST termed
   a(n)
       A. administrative assistant   B. assistant to
       C. staff assistant   D. staff specialist

8. In organizing, doing what *works* in the particular situa-   8.___
   tion, with due regard to both short and long range objectives, is BEST termed
       A. ambivalence   B. authoritarianism
       C. decentralization   D. pragmatism

9. If an effort were made to reduce the number of private   9.___
   offices in a new layout, the LEAST effective substitute
   in offering privacy would be the use of
       A. an open area with lower movable partitions or
          railings separating each individual
       B. conference rooms
       C. larger desks
       D. modular desk units

10. The term *administrative substation* NORMALLY refers to   10.___
       A. a work station handling a number of office services
          for an office organization
       B. a work station where middle level supervisors are
          located
       C. an office for handling management trainees
       D. the functions allocated to particular levels of
          administrative managers

11. An operations research technique which would be applied   11.___
    to determine the optimum number of window clerks or inter-
    viewers to have in an agency serving the public would MOST
    likely be the use of
       A. line of balance   B. queuing theory
       C. simulation   D. work sampling

12. A type of file which permits the operator to remain   12.___
    seated while the file can be moved backward and forward
    as required is BEST termed a ____ file.
       A. lateral   B. movable
       C. reciprocating   D. rotary

13. The technique of work measurement in which the analyst
    observes the work at random times of the day is BEST
    termed
    A. indirect observation   B. logging
    C. ratio delay   D. wristwatch

13.___

14. Examples of predetermined time systems generally should
    include all of the following EXCEPT
    A. Master Clerical Data   B. Methods Time Measurement
    C. Short Interval Data   D. Work Factor

14.___

15. A technique by which the supervisor or an assistant
    distributes a predetermined batch of work to the employees
    at periodic intervals of the day is generally BEST known as
    A. backlog control scheduling
    B. production control scheduling
    C. short interval scheduling
    D. workload balancing

15.___

16. E. Wright Bakke defined his *fusion process* as: The
    A. work environment to some degree remakes the organiza-
       tion and the organization to some degree remakes the
       work environment
    B. fusing of the interests of both management and labor
       unions
    C. community of interest between first line supervisors
       and top management
    D. organization to some degree remakes the individual
       and the individual to some degree remakes the
       organization

16.___

17. The title of a recent best-selling book by Robert
    Townsend is:
    A. MANAGEMENT ANALYSIS: WAVE OF THE FUTURE
    B. MANAGEMENT FOR RESULTS
    C. THE HUMAN SIDE OF ENTERPRISE
    D. UP THE ORGANIZATION

17.___

18. In planning office space for a newly established bureau,
    it would usually be LEAST desirable to
    A. concentrate, rather than disperse, the chief sources
       of office noises
    B. design an office environment with about the same
       brightness as the office desk
    C. designate as reception rooms, washrooms and other
       service areas those areas that will receive lesser
       amounts of illumination than those areas in which
       private office work will be performed
    D. eliminate natural light in cases where it is not
       the major light source

18.___

19. A private office should be used when its use is dictated
    by facts and unbiased judgment. It should never be pro-
    vided simply because requests and sometimes pressure have
    been brought to bear.

19.___

Of the following reasons used to justify use of a private
office, the one that requires the MOST care in determining
whether a private office is actually warranted is
   A. an office has always been provided for a particular
      job
   B. prestige considerations
   C. the confidential nature of the work
   D. the work involves high concentration

20. Theoretically, an ideal organization structure can be set   20.____
    up for each enterprise. In actual practice, the ideal
    organization structure is seldom, if ever, obtained.
    Of the following, the one that normally is of LEAST influ-
    ence in determining the organization structure is the
       A. existence of agreements and favors among members
          of the organization
       B. funds available
       C. opinions and beliefs of top executives
       D. tendency of management to discard established forms
          in favor of new forms

21. An IMPORTANT aspect to keep in mind during the decision-   21.____
    making process is that
       A. all possible alternatives for attaining goals should
          be sought out and considered
       B. considering various alternatives only leads to
          confusion
       C. once a decision has been made, it cannot be retracted
       D. there is only one correct method to reach any goal

22. Implementation of accountability requires   22.____
       A. a leader who will not hesitate to take punitive action
       B. an established system of communication from the
          bottom to the top
       C. explicit directives from leaders
       D. too much expense to justify it

23. Of the following, the MAJOR difference between systems   23.____
    and procedures analysis and work simplification is:
       A. The former complicates organizational routine and
          the latter simplifies it
       B. The former is objective and the latter is subjective
       C. The former generally utilizes expert advice and the
          latter is a *do-it-yourself* improvement by super-
          visors and workers
       D. There is no difference other than in name

24. Systems development is concerned with providing   24.____
       A. a specific set of work procedures
       B. an overall framework to describe general relationships
       C. definitions of particular organizational functions
       D. organizational symbolism

25. Organizational systems and procedures should be
    A. developed as problems arise as no design can anticipate adequately the requirements of an organization
    B. developed jointly by experts in systems and procedures and the people who are responsible for implementing them
    C. developed solely by experts in systems and procedures
    D. eliminated whenever possible to save unnecessary expense

25.____

_____

KEY (CORRECT ANSWERS)

1. D		11. B	
2. A		12. C	
3. B		13. C	
4. D		14. C	
5. D		15. C	
6. B		16. D	
7. D		17. D	
8. D		18. D	
9. C		19. A	
10. A		20. D	

21. A
22. B
23. C
24. B
25. B

_____

TEST 3

1. The CHIEF danger of a decentralized control system is that
    A. excessive reports and communications will be generated
    B. problem areas may not be detected readily
    C. the expense will become prohibitive
    D. this will result in too many *chiefs*

    1.___

2. Of the following, management guides and controls clerical work PRINCIPALLY through
    A. close supervision and constant checking of personnel
    B. spot checking of clerical procedures
    C. strong sanctions for clerical supervisors
    D. the use of printed forms

    2.___

3. Which of the following is MOST important before conducting fact-finding interviews?
    A. Becoming acquainted with all personnel to be interviewed
    B. Explaining the techniques you plan to use
    C. Explaining to the operating officials the purpose and scope of the study
    D. Orientation of the physical layout

    3.___

4. Of the following, the one that is NOT essential in carrying out a comprehensive work improvement program is
    A. standards of performance   B. supervisory training
    C. work count/task list   D. work distribution chart

    4.___

5. Which of the following control techniques is MOST useful on large complex systems projects?
    A. A general work plan   B. Cantt chart
    C. Monthly progress report D. PERT chart

    5.___

6. The action which is MOST effective in gaining acceptance of a study by the agency which is being studied is
    A. a directive from the agency head to install a study based on recommendations included in a report
    B. a lecture-type presentation following approval of the procedures
    C. a written procedure in narrative form covering the proposed system with visual presentations and discussions
    D. procedural charts showing the *before* situation, forms, steps, etc. to the employees affected

    6.___

7. Which of the following is NOT an advantage in the use of   7.___
   oral instructions as compared with written instructions?
   Oral instruction(s)
   A. can easily be changed
   B. is superior in transmitting complex directives
   C. facilitate exchange of information between a superior
      and his subordinate
   D. with discussions make it easier to ascertain under-
      standing

8. Which organization principle is MOST closely related to   8.___
   procedural analysis and improvement?
   A. Duplication, overlapping, and conflict should be
      eliminated.
   B. Managerial authority should be clearly defined.
   C. The objectives of the organization should be clearly
      defined.
   D. Top management should be freed of burdensome detail.

9. Which one of the following is the MAJOR objective of   9.___
   operational audits?
   A. Detecting fraud
   B. Determining organization problems
   C. Determining the number of personnel needed
   D. Recommending opportunities for improving operating
      and management practices

10. Of the following, the formalization of organization   10.___
    structure is BEST achieved by
    A. a narrative description of the plan of organization
    B. functional charts
    C. job descriptions together with organization charts
    D. multi-flow charts

11. Budget planning is MOST useful when it achieves   11.___
    A. cost control   B. forecast of receipts
    C. performance review   D. personnel reduction

12. The UNDERLYING principle of sound administration is to   12.___
    A. base administration on investigation of facts
    B. have plenty of resources available
    C. hire a strong administrator
    D. establish a broad policy

13. Although questionnaires are not the best survey tool the   13.___
    management analyst has to use, there are times when a
    good questionnaire can expedite the *fact-finding* phase
    of a management survey.
    Which of the following should be AVOIDED in the design
    and distribution of the questionnaire?
    A. Questions should be framed so that answers can be
       classified and tabulated for analysis.
    B. Those receiving the questionnaire must be knowledge-
       able enough to accurately provide the information
       desired.

    C. The questionnaire should enable the respondent to
       answer in a narrative manner.
    D. The questionnaire should require a minimum amount
       of writing.

14. Of the following, the formula which is used to calculate
the arithmetic mean from data grouped in a frequency
distribution is:

    A. $M = \dfrac{N}{\Sigma f\chi}$ B. $M = N(\Sigma f\chi)$ C. $M = \dfrac{\Sigma f\chi}{N}$ D. $M = \dfrac{\Sigma \chi}{fN}$

14.____

15. Arranging large groups of numbers in frequency distribu-
tions
    A. gives a more composite picture of the total group
       than a random listing
    B. is misleading in most cases
    C. is unnecessary in most instances
    D. presents the data in a form whereby further manipula-
       tion of the group is eliminated

15.____

16. After a budget has been developed, it serves to
    A. assist the accounting department in posting
       expenditures
    B. measure the effectiveness of department managers
    C. provide a yardstick against which actual costs are
       measured
    D. provide the operating department with total expendi-
       tures to date

16.____

17. Of the following, which formula is used to determine
staffing requirements?
    A. $\dfrac{\text{Hours per man-day}}{\text{Volume X Standard}}$ = Employees Needed

    B. $\dfrac{\text{Hours per man-day X Standard}}{\text{Volume}}$ = Employees Needed

    C. $\dfrac{\text{Hours per man-day X Volume}}{\text{Standard}}$ = Employees Needed

    D. $\dfrac{\text{Volume X Standard}}{\text{Hours per man-day}}$ = Employees Needed

17.____

18. Of the following, which formula is used to determine the
number of days required to process work?
    A. $\dfrac{\text{Employees X Daily Output}}{\text{Volume}}$ = Days to Process Work

    B. $\dfrac{\text{Employees X Volume}}{\text{Daily Output}}$ = Days to Process Work

    C. $\dfrac{\text{Volume}}{\text{Employees X Daily Output}}$ = Days to Process Work

    D. $\dfrac{\text{Volume X Daily Output}}{\text{Employees}}$ = Days to Process Work

18.____

19. Identify this symbol, as used in a Systems Flow Chart.   19.___

    A. Document   B. Decision   C. Preparation D. Process

20. Of the following, the MAIN advantage of a form letter   20.___
over a dictated letter is that a form letter
    A. is more expressive
    B. is neater
    C. may be mailed in a window envelope
    D. requires less secretarial time

21. The term that may be defined as *a systematic analysis of*   21.___
all factors affecting work being done or all factors that
will affect work to be done, in order to save effort, time,
or money is
    A. flow process charting   B. work flow analysis
    C. work measurement   D. work simplification

22. Generally, the LEAST important basic factor to be con-   22.___
sidered in developing office layout improvements is to
locate
    A. office equipment, reference facilities, and files as
       close as practicable to those using them
    B. persons as close as practicable to the persons from
       whom they receive their work
    C. persons as close as practicable to windows and/or
       adequate ventilation
    D. persons who are friendly with each other close
       together to improve morale

23. Of the following, the one which is LEAST effective in   23.___
reducing administrative costs is
    A. applying objective measurement techniques to deter-
       mine the time required to perform a given task
    B. establishing budgets on the basis of historical
       performance data
    C. motivating supervisors and managers in the importance
       of cost reduction
    D. selecting the best method -- manual, mechanical, or
       electronic -- to process the essential work

24. *Fire-fighting* is a common expression in management   24.___
terminology.
Of the following, which BEST describes *fire-fighting* as
an analyst's approach to solving paperwork problems?
    A. A complete review of all phases of the department's
       processing functions
    B. A studied determination of the proper equipment to
       process the work

C. An analysis of each form that is being processed
   and the logical reasons for its processing
D. The solution of problems as they arise, usually
   at the request of operating personnel

25. Assume that an analyst with a proven record of accomplish- 25.___
    ment on many projects is having difficulties on his
    present assignment.
    Of the following, the BEST course of action for his
    superior to take is to
    A. assume there is a personality conflict involved and
       transfer the analyst to another project
    B. give the analyst some time off
    C. review the nature of the project to determine whether
       or not the analyst is equipped to handle the assign-
       ment
    D. suggest that the analyst seek counseling

KEY (CORRECT ANSWERS)

1. B		11. A	
2. D		12. A	
3. C		13. C	
4. B		14. C	
5. D		15. A	
6. C		16. C	
7. B		17. D	
8. A		18. C	
9. D		19. A	
10. C		20. D	

21. D
22. D
23. B
24. D
25. C

EXAMINATION SECTION
TEST 1

DIRECTIONS: Each question or incomplete statement is followed by
several suggested answers or completions. Select the
one that BEST answers the question or completes the
statement. *PRINT THE LETTER OF THE CORRECT ANSWER IN
THE SPACE AT THE RIGHT.*

1. With a management staff of 15 capable analysts, which of   1.____
    the following organizational approaches would generally
    be BEST for overall results?
    Organization
    A. by specialists in fields, such as management,
       organization, systems analysis
    B. by clientele to be served, such as hospitals, police,
       education, social services
    C. where all 15 report directly to head of the manage-
       ment staff
    D. by specialized study groups with flexibility in
       assigning staff under a qualified project leader

2. In conducting a general management survey to identify   2.____
    problems and opportunities, which of the following would
    it be LEAST necessary to consider?
    A. Identifying program and planning deficiencies in
       each functional area
    B. Organization problems
    C. Sound management practices not being used
    D. The qualifications of the supervisory personnel

3. Which of the following statements MOST accurately defines   3.____
    operations research?
    A. A highly sophisticated system used in the analysis of
       management problems
    B. A specialized application of electronic data pro-
       cessing in the analysis of management problems
    C. Research on operating problems
    D. The application of sophisticated mathematical tools
       to the analysis of management problems

4. Theoretically, an ideal organization structure can be   4.____
    set up for each enterprise. In actual practice, the
    ideal organization structure is seldom, if ever, obtained.
    Of the following, the one that is of LEAST influence in
    determining the organization structure is the
    A. existence of agreements and favors among members of
       the organization
    B. funds available
    C. growing trend of management to discard established
       forms in favor of new forms
    D. opinions and beliefs of top executives

5. To which one of the following is it MOST important that the functional or technical staff specialist in a large organization devote major attention?   5.___
   A. Conducting audits of line operations
   B. Controlling of people in the line organization
   C. Developing improved approaches, plans, and procedures and assisting the line organization in their implementation
   D. Providing advice to his superior and to operating units

6. In the planning for reorganization of a department, which one of the following principles relating to the assignment of functions is NOT correct?   6.___
   A. Line and staff functions should be separated.
   B. Separate functions should be assigned to separate organizational units.
   C. There should be no disturbance of the previously assigned tasks of personnel.
   D. There should generally be no overlapping among organizational elements.

7. Results are BEST accomplished within an organization when the budgets and plans are developed by the   7.___
   A. budget office, independent of the operating units
   B. head of the operating unit based on analysis of prior year's operations after discussion with his superior
   C. head of the operating unit with general guidelines and data from higher authority and the budget office, and input from key personnel
   D. head of the organization unit based on an analysis of prior year's operations

8. The *management process* is a term used to describe the responsibilities common to   8.___
   A. all levels of management
   B. first line supervisors
   C. middle management jobs
   D. top management jobs

9. Of the following, committees are BEST used for   9.___
   A. advising the head of the organization
   B. improving functional work
   C. making executive decisions
   D. making specific planning decisions

10. Which of the following would NOT be a part of a management control system?   10.___
    A. An objective test of new ideas or methods in operation
    B. Determination of need for organization improvement
    C. Objective comparison of operating results
    D. Provision of information useful for revising objectives, programs, and operations

11. Of the following, the one which a line role generally   11.___
    does NOT include is
    A. controlling results and performance
    B. coordinating work and exchanging ideas with other
       line organizations
    C. implementation of approved plans developed by staff
    D. planning work and making operating decisions

12. In a normal curve, one standard deviation would include   12.___
    MOST NEARLY what percentage of the cases involved?
    A. 50%   B. 68%   C. 95%   D. 99%

13. The Office Layout Chart is a sketch of the physical   13.___
    arrangements of the office to which has been added the
    flow lines of the principal work performed there.
    Which one of the following states the BEST advantage of
    superimposing the work flow onto the desk layout?
    A. Lighting and acoustics can be improved.
    B. Line and staff relationships can be determined.
    C. Obvious misarrangements can be corrected.
    D. The number of delays can be determined.

14. An advantage of the Multiple Process Chart over the Flow 14.___
    Process Chart is that the Multiple Process Chart shows
    the
    A. individual worker's activity
    B. number of delays
    C. sequence of operations
    D. simultaneous flow of work in several departments

15. Of the following, which is the MAJOR advantage of a   15.___
    microfilm record retention system?
    A. Filing can follow the terminal digit system.
    B. Retrieving documents from the files is faster.
    C. Significant space is saved in storing records.
    D. To read a microfilm record, a film reader is not
       necessary.

16. Which one of the following questions should the manage-   16.___
    ment analyst generally consider FIRST?
    A. How is it being done? and Why should it be done
       that way?
    B. What is being done? and Why is it necessary?
    C. When should this job be done? and Why?
    D. Who should do the job? and Why should he do it?

17. Assume that you are in the process of eliminating unneces- 17.___
    sary forms.
    The answer to which one of the following questions would
    be LEAST relevant?
    A. Could the information be obtained elsewhere?
    B. Is the form properly designed?
    C. Is the form used as intended?
    D. Is the purpose of the form essential to the operation?

18. Use of color in forms adds to their cost. Sometimes,
    however, the use of color will greatly simplify procedure
    and more than pay for itself in time saved and errors
    eliminated.
    This is ESPECIALLY true when
    A. a form passes through many reviewers
    B. considerable sorting is required
    C. the form is other than a standard size
    D. the form will not be sent through the mail

18.___

19. Of the following techniques, the one GENERALLY employed
    and considered BEST in forms design is to divide writing
    lines into boxes with captions printed in small type
    _____ of the box.
    A. centered in the lower part
    B. centered in the upper part
    C. in the upper lefthand corner
    D. in the lower righthand corner

19.___

20. Many forms authorities advocate the construction of a
    functional forms file or index.
    If such a file is set up, the MOST effective way of
    classifying forms for such an index is classification by
    A. department
    B. form number
    C. name or type of form
    D. subject to which the form applies

20.___

21. An interrelated pattern of jobs which makes up the
    structure of a system is known as
    A. a chain of command
    B. cybernetics
    C. the formal organization
    D. the maintenance pattern

21.___

22. A transparent sheet of film containing multiple rows of
    microimages is characteristic of which one of the follow-
    ing types of microfilm?
    A. Aperture   B. Jacket
    C. Microfiche   D. Roll or reel

22.___

23. PRIMARY responsibility for training and development of
    employees generally rests with
    A. outside training agencies
    B. the individual who needs training
    C. the line supervisor
    D. the training specialist in the Personnel Office

23.___

24. Which of the following approaches usually provides the
    BEST communication in the objectives and values of a new
    program which is to be introduced?
    A. A general written description of the program by the
       program manager for review by those who share
       responsibility

24.___

    B. An effective verbal presentation by the program
       manager to those affected
    C. Development of the plan and operational approach
       in carrying out the program by the program manager
       assisted by his key subordinates
    D. Development of the plan by the program manager's
       supervisor

25. The term *total systems concept*, as used in electronic   25.___
     data processing, refers
    A. only to the computer and its associated electronic
       accessories
    B. only to the paper information output, or *software*
       aspect
    C. to a large computer-based information handling
       system, which supplies the information needs of an
       entire agency or corporation
    D. to all of the automated and manual information
       systems in a specific sub-division of an organiza-
       tion

26. Of the following, scientific management can BEST be   26.___
     considered as an attempt to establish work procedures
    A. in fields of scientific endeavors
    B. which are beneficial only to bosses
    C. which require less control
    D. utilizing the concept of a man-machine system

27. The MAJOR failing of efficiency engineering was that it   27.___
    A. overlooked the human factor
    B. required experts to implement the techniques
    C. was not based on true scientific principles
    D. was too costly and time consuming

28. Which of the following organizations is MOST noted   28.___
     throughout the world for its training in management?
    A. American Management Association
    B. American Political Science Association
    C. Society for the Advancement of Management
    D. Systems and Procedures Association

29. The GENERAL method of arriving at program objectives   29.___
     should be
    A. a trial and error process
    B. developed as the program progresses
    C. included in the program plan
    D. left to the discretion of the immediate supervisors

30. The review and appraisal of an organization to determine   30.___
     waste and deficiencies, improved methods, better means
     of control, more efficient operations, and greater use of
     human and physical facilities is known as a(n)
    A. management audit
    B. manpower survey
    C. work simplification study
    D. operations audit

31. When data are grouped into a frequency distribution, the
    median is BEST defined as the _____ in the distribution.
    A. 50% point
    B. largest single range
    C. smallest single range
    D. point of greatest concentration

31.____

32. The manual, visual, and mental elements into which an
    operation may be analyzed in time and motion study are
    denoted by the term
    A. measurement   B. positioning
    C. standards   D. therbligs

32.____

33. Of the following, the symbol shown at
    the right, as used in a systems flow
    chart, denotes
    A. decision
    B. document
    C. manual operation
    D. process

33.____

34. Of the following agencies of city government, the one
    with the LARGEST expense budget for the current fiscal
    year is the
    A. environmental protection administration
    B. department of social services
    C. municipal service administration
    D. police department

34.____

35. A feasibility study is the first phase in the process
    of conversion from manual to computerized data process-
    ing.
    The phases, in sequence, are the feasibility study,
    A. system conversion, system installation,
       follow up
    B. system design, installation
    C. system design, follow up, installation
    D. system design, system conversion, installation

35.____

36.

36.____

NAME OF WORKER	1st Hour	2nd Hour	3rd Hour	4th Hour	5th Hour	6th Hour	7th Hour	8th Hour	
J. Jones									
B. Brown									
R. Roe									

The type of chart illustrated above is generally known
as a _____ Chart.
    A. Flow   B. Gantt
    C. Work Simplification   D. Motion-Time Study

37.

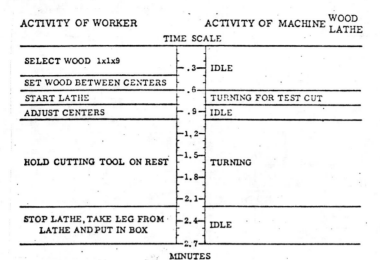

The type of chart illustrated above is generally known as a _____ Chart.

A. Flow
B. Gantt
C. Simo
D. Work Simplification

37.___

38.

The type of chart illustrated above is generally known as a(n) _____ Chart.

A. Multiple Activity
B. Motion-Time
C. Work Place Layout
D. Operation Process

38.___

39.   39.___

The one illustrated above is generally known as a
- A. Gantt Chart
- B. Multiple Activity Chart
- C. Planned Flow Diagram
- D. Work Place Diagram

40.   40.___

	PRESENT		PROPOSED		DIFFERENCE	
	No.	Time	No.	Time	No.	Time
OPERATIONS						
TRANSPORTATIONS						
INSPECTIONS						
DELAYS						
STORAGES						
DISTANCE TRAVELLED		Ft.		Ft.		Ft.

JOB

CHART BEGINS
CHART ENDS
CHARTED BY
DATE

DETAILS OF PRESENT / PROPOSED METHOD	OPERATION TRANSPORT INSPECTION DELAY STORAGE	DISTANCE BY FEET	TIME BY MINUTES	DETAILS OF PRESENT / PROPOSED METHOD	OPERATION TRANSPORT INSPECTION DELAY STORAGE	DISTANCE BY FEET	TIME IN MINUTES
1.	O ⇨ □ D ▽			1.	O ⇨ □ D ▽		
2.	O ⇨ □ D ▽			2.	O ⇨ □ D ▽		
3.	O ⇨ □ D ▽			3.	O ⇨ □ D ▽		
4.	O ⇨ □ D ▽			4.	O ⇨ □ D ▽		
5.	O ⇨ □ D ▽			5.	O ⇨ □ D ▽		
6.	O ⇨ □ D ▽			6.	O ⇨ □ D ▽		
7.	O ⇨ □ D ▽			7.	O ⇨ □ D ▽		
8.	O ⇨ □ D ▽			8.	O ⇨ □ D ▽		

The type of chart illustrated above is generally known
as a(n) _____ Chart.
   A. Analysis   B. Flow Process
   C. Man or Material   D. Multiple Activity

———

KEY (CORRECT ANSWERS)

1. D	11. B	21. C	31. A
2. D	12. B	22. C	32. D
3. D	13. C	23. C	33. A
4. C	14. D	24. C	34. B
5. C	15. C	25. C	35. D
6. C	16. B	26. D	36. B
7. C	17. B	27. A	37. C
8. A	18. B	28. A	38. D
9. A	19. C	29. C	39. C
10. B	20. D	30. A	40. B

———

TEST 2

1. The one of the following which is MOST important in get-   1.___
ting a systems survey off to a good start is
   A. a kick-off meeting with key personnel covering the
      purpose of the study and introduction of the survey
      staff
   B. a prior knowledge of the organization manual, charts,
      and statements of responsibility
   C. knowledge of personality problems in the agency
      needing special attention
   D. written announcement from the agency head

2. Which of the following is the LEAST important factor in   2.___
planning an administrative survey?
   A. Developing a work plan and time schedule
   B. Knowledge of sound organization concepts and prin-
      ciples
   C. Survey techniques and methods to be used for analysis
      in compiling data needed
   D. The purpose, scope, and level of the survey

3. Assume that a supervisor, when reviewing a decision   3.___
reached by one of his subordinates, finds the decision
incorrect.
Under these circumstances, it would be MOST desirable
for the supervisor to
   A. correct the decision and inform the subordinate of
      this at a staff meeting
   B. correct the decision and suggest a more detailed
      analysis in the future
   C. help the employee find the reason for the correct
      decision
   D. refrain from assigning this type of problem to the
      employee

4. After an analyst has identified a problem area, which one   4.___
of the following is the MOST important step in getting
management to recognize that a problem does exist?
   A. A brief statement describing the problem
   B. Implications if problem is not corrected
   C. Relationship to other problems
   D. Supporting factual evidence and data indicating that
      the problem does exist

5. The statement, *work expands to fit the time available for its completion*, refers MOST directly to
   A. job enlargement principles
   B. Parkinson's Law
   C. The Open System Theory
   D. The Peter Principle

   5.___

6. A comprehensive and constructive examination of a company, institution, or branch of government, or of any of its components such as an agency, division, or department, and its plans and objectives, methods of control, its means of operations, and its use of human and physical facilities is COMMONLY known as a(n) _____ audit.
   A. systems
   B. extensive financial
   C. operational or management
   D. organizational

   6.___

7. Assume you are assigned to analyze the details of the procedures a clerk follows in order to complete filling out an invoice or a requisition. Your purpose is to simplify and shorten the procedure he has been trained to use.
   The MOST appropriate chart for this purpose would be the
   A. block flow diagram   B. flow process chart
   C. forms flow chart   D. work distribution chart

   7.___

8. In identifying problems and opportunities for improvement, which one of the following is MOST closely related to organization planning?
   A. Effective operating procedures issued from headquarters
   B. Effective records management
   C. Need for improved management concepts and practices
   D. Review of the salary and wage administration program

   8.___

9. MOST of the working time of the functional or technical staff specialist in a large organization should be focused on
   A. conducting audits of line operations
   B. developing improved approaches, plans, and procedures and assisting the line organization in their implementation
   C. providing advice to his superior and to operating units
   D. the number of people in the line organization

   9.___

10. The LEAST effective way for a survey group to plan is to
    A. clarify objectives and identify problems
    B. conduct planning and review sessions annually when budgets are prepared
    C. periodically conduct review sessions for purposes of coordination
    D. undertake specific action programs

    10.___

11. Which one of the following is the MOST important element   11.___
    of a good manpower plan?
    A. Establishing inventories of capable personnel
    B. Forecasting the number of people needed in the future
    C. Having the right people for all jobs when needed
    D. Identifying training needs

12. Completed staff work is MOST effective in accomplishing   12.___
    which one of the following?
    A. Determination of the problems of the line organiza-
       tion
    B. Determination of the staffing needs of an organiza-
       tion
    C. Preparation of effective proposals and approaches to
       improve line results
    D. Review of budgets proposed by line organization

13. What generally is the PRINCIPAL objection to the use of   13.___
    form letters?
    The
    A. difficulty of developing a form letter to serve the
       purpose
    B. excessive time involved in selecting the proper form
       letter
    C. errors in selecting form letters
    D. impersonality of form letters

14. What is the BEST approach for introducing change?   14.___
    A
    A. combination of written and also verbal communication
       to all personnel affected by the change
    B. general bulletin to all personnel
    C. meeting pointing out all the values of the new
       approach
    D. written directive to key personnel

15. The FIRST step in designing an effective management survey 15.___
    is
    A. examining backlogs
    B. flow charting
    C. motion analysis and time study
    D. project planning

16. In statistical sampling, the error which will NOT be   16.___
    exceeded by 50 percent of the cases is known as the
    A. difference between two means
    B. probable error
    C. standard deviation
    D. standard error of the mean

17. In a normal or bell-shaped curve, the area encompassed   17.___
    by two standard deviations from the mean is
    A. 68%   B. 95%   C. 97%   D. 99%

18. The statistical average referring to that point on the   18.___
    scale at which the concentration is greatest or that value
    which occurs the greatest number of times and which might
    be taken as typical of the entire distribution is called
    the
       A. mean   B. median   C. mode   D. quartile

19. In process charting, the symbol which is used when con-   19.___
    ditions (except those which intentionally change the
    physical or chemical characteristics of the object) do
    not permit or require immediate performance is

    A. □   B. ○   C. ▷   D. ▽

20. Assume that you are making a study of a central head-   20.___
    quarters office which processes claims received from a
    number of district offices. You notice the following
    problems: Some employees are usually busy, while others
    doing the same kind of work in the same grade have little
    to do, high level professional people frequently spend
    considerable time searching for files in the file room.
    Which of the following charts would be MOST useful to
    record and analyze the data needed to help solve these
    problems?
    _____ Chart.
       A. Forms Distribution   B. Process
       C. Space Layout   D. Work Distribution

21. Which of the following types of work would NOT be readily   21.___
    measured by conventional time study techniques?
    Work
       A. of sufficient volume, uniform in nature, that will
          justify the cost of continuing and maintaining
          controls
       B. that is countable in precise quantitative terms
       C. that is essentially creative and considerably
          varied in content
       D. that is repetitive, uniform, and homogeneous in
          content over a period of time

22. Which of the following should be the FIRST consideration   22.___
    in a work simplification study?
    Can the
       A. sequence be changed for improvement?
       B. task be combined with another?
       C. task be eliminated?
       D. task be simplified?

23. In evaluating the sequence of operations involved in   23.___
    the clerical processing, which of the items listed below
    would be an indicator that methods improvements are
    needed?
    A. Some operations duplicate previous operations.
    B. The supervisor believes many of the company's
       policies are wrong.
    C. There is a high turnover of mail clerks.
    D. Work is logged into and out of the department.

24. Of the following, the one that is MOST likely to make a   24.___
    methods change unacceptable is when the
    A. change does not threaten the workers' security
    B. change follows a series of previously unsuccessful
       similar changes
    C. change has been well thought out and properly intro-
       duced
    D. people affected by the change have participated in
       the development of the changes

25. Which of the following questions has the LEAST signifi-   25.___
    cant bearing on the analysis of the paperwork flow?
    A. How is the work brought into the department and how
       is it taken away?
    B. How many work stations are involved in processing
       the work within the department?
    C. Is the work received and removed in the proper
       quantity?
    D. Where is the supervisor's desk located in relation-
       ship to those he supervises?

26. Which of the following does NOT have significant bearing   26.___
    on the arrangement, sequence, and zoning of information
    into box captions?
    The
    A. layout of the source documents from which the infor-
       mation is taken
    B. logical flow of data
    C. needs of forms to be prepared from this form
    D. type of print to be employed

27. In determining the spacing requirements of a form and   27.___
    the size of the boxes to be used, PRIMARY consideration
    should be given to the
    A. distribution of the form
    B. method of entry, i.e., handwritten or machine and
       type of machine
    C. number of copies
    D. number of items to be entered

28. Of the following, the BEST technique to follow when   28.___
    providing instructions for the completion and routing
    of a form is to _____ the form.

A. imprint the instructions on the face of
B. imprint the instructions on the back of
C. provide a written procedure to accompany
D. provide verbal instructions when issuing

29. A forms layout style where a separate space in the shape   29.___
of a box is provided for each item of information requested and the caption or question for each item is
shown in the upper lefthand corner of each box is known
as the _____ style.
   A. box   B. checkbox
   C. checklist   D. checkbox and checklist

30. It is the office manager's responsibility to promote   30.___
office safety and eliminate hazards. A number of policies
and procedures are widely advocated and followed by
management and safety experts.
Of the following, the policy or procedure that is LEAST
valid is:
   A. Each department supervisor should be required to
      complete a report at the time of each accident so
      that the person in charge of safety administration
      will be able to analyze the pattern of common
      causes and improve safety conditions
   B. Electrical cords and connectors for machines and
      equipment should be routinely checked so as to
      eliminate fire and shock hazards
   C. Employees should be informed of the type of acci-
      dents which may occur
   D. Smoking at desks should be prohibited so as to avoid
      the possibility of fire hazards; and a lounge
      provided for this purpose

31. An effective discussion leader is one who   31.___
   A. announces the problem and his preconceived solution
      at the start of the discussion
   B. guides and directs the discussion according to pre-
      arranged outline
   C. interrupts or corrects confused participants to save
      time
   D. permits anyone to say anything at anytime

32. Under what circumstances would it be MOST advisable to   32.___
have two or more clerks in a department share the same
adding machine?
When
   A. capital appropriations are tight
   B. the clerks sharing the adding machine are located
      at adjacent desks
   C. the clerks sharing the adding machine get along
      with one another
   D. the need for the equipment is so little that there
      is negligible time lost in sharing the adding machine

33. Of the following, the statement that is MOST descriptive   33.____
    of, and fundamental to, proper office landscaping is:
    A. All clerical desks should be arranged singly and
       in rows
    B. The layout should be built around the flow of infor-
       mation and work in the office
    C. The layout should be built around the recognized
       organizational hierarchy of the office unit
    D. There should be many planters arranged to give the
       office an open look

34. The MOST significant factor to be considered in deciding   34.____
    on an electric typewriter is the
    A. ability of some electric typewriters to change type
       face
    B. prestige typists associate with an electric type-
       writer
    C. standardization of type face
    D. volume of work to be performed by the typist

35. The human relations movement in management theory is   35.____
    BASICALLY concerned with
    A. counteracting employee unrest
    B. eliminating the *time and motion* man
    C. interrelationships among individuals in organizations
    D. the psychology of the worker

36. PERT, as commonly used, stood for   36.____
    A. Periodic Estimate of Resource Trends
    B. Potential Energy Research Technology
    C. Professional Engineer Review Tests
    D. Program Evaluation and Review Technique

37. The BEST type of chart to use in showing the absolute   37.____
    movement or change of a continuous series of data over
    a period of time, such as changes in prices, employment
    or expenses, is usually a _____ chart.
    A. bar   B. line
    C. multiple bar   D. pie

38. A computer language that was ESPECIALLY designed for   38.____
    third generation computers to enable their capabilities
    to be effectively utilized is
    A. BASIC   B. COBOL   C. FORTRAN   D. PL/1

39. An analog computer computes by making measurements on   39.____
    A. a storage drum
    B. magnetic tape
    C. punched cards
    D. some parallel physical system

40. The ONLY basic arithmetic operations performed by digital   40.___
    computers are
        A. addition and subtraction
        B. addition, subtraction, multiplication, and division
        C. exponential equations
        D. multiplication and division

KEY (CORRECT ANSWERS)

1. A	11. C	21. C	31. B
2. B	12. C	22. C	32. D
3. C	13. D	23. A	33. B
4. D	14. A	24. B	34. D
5. B	15. D	25. D	35. C
6. C	16. B	26. D	36. D
7. B	17. B	27. B	37. B
8. C	18. C	28. A	38. D
9. B	19. C	29. A	39. D
10. B	20. D	30. D	40. A

READING COMPREHENSION
UNDERSTANDING AND INTERPRETING WRITTEN MATERIAL

EXAMINATION SECTION

DIRECTIONS: Each question or incomplete statement is followed by several suggested answers or completions. Select the one that BEST answers the question or completes the statement. *PRINT THE LETTER OF THE CORRECT ANSWER IN THE SPACE AT THE RIGHT.*

TEST 1

Questions 1-2.

DIRECTIONS: Questions 1 and 2 are to be answered SOLELY on the basis of the following passage.

The employees in a unit or division of a government agency may be referred to as a work group. Within a government agency which has existed for some time, the work groups will have evolved traditions of their own. The persons in these work groups acquire these traditions as part of the process of work adjustment within their groups. Usually, a work group in a large organization will contain *oldtimers*, *newcomers*, and *in-betweeners*. Like the supervisor of a group, who is not necessarily an oldtimer or the oldest member, oldtimers usually have great influence. They can recall events unknown to others and are a storehouse of information and advice about current problems in the light of past experience. They pass along the traditions of the group to the others who, in turn, become oldtimers themselves. Thus, the traditions of the group which have been honored and revered by long acceptance are continued.

1. According to the above passage, the traditions of a work group within a government agency are developed
   A. at the time the group is established
   B. over a considerable period of time
   C. in order to give recognition to oldtimers
   D. for the group before it is established

1.___

2. According to the above passage, the oldtimers within a work group
   A. are the means by which long accepted practices and customs are perpetuated
   B. would best be able to settle current problems that arise
   C. are honored because of the changes they have made in the traditions
   D. have demonstrated that they have learned to do their work well

2.___

Questions 3-4.

DIRECTIONS: Questions 3 and 4 are to be answered SOLELY on the basis of the following passage.

In public agencies, the success of a person assigned to perform first-line supervisory duties depends in large part upon the personal relations between him and his subordinate employees. The goal of supervising effort is something more than to obtain compliance with procedures established by some central office. The major objective is work accomplishment. In order for this goal to be attained, employees must want to attain it and must exercise initiative in their work. Only if employees are generally satisfied with the type of supervision which exists in an organization will they put forth their best efforts.

3. According to the above passage, in order for employees to   3.___
    try to do their work as well as they can, it is essential
    that
        A. they participate in determining their working conditions
           and rates of pay
        B. their supervisors support the employees' viewpoints in
           meetings with higher management
        C. they are content with the supervisory practices which
           are being used
        D. their supervisors make the changes in working proce-
           dures that the employees request

4. It can be inferred from the above passage that the goals   4.___
    of a unit in a public agency will not be reached unless
    the employees in the unit
        A. wish to reach them and are given the opportunity to
           make individual contributions to the work
        B. understand the relationship between the goals of the
           unit and goals of the agency
        C. have satisfactory personal relationships with employees
           of other units in the agency
        D. carefully follow the directions issued by higher
           authorities

Questions 5-9.

DIRECTIONS: Questions 5 through 9 are to be answered SOLELY on the
              basis of the following passage.

    If an employee thinks he can save money, time, or material for the city or has an idea about how to do something better than it is being done, he shouldn't keep it to himself. He should send his ideas to the Employee's Suggestion Program, using the special form which is kept on hand in all departments. An employee may send in as many ideas as he wishes. To make sure that each idea is judged fairly, the name of the suggester is not made known until an award is made. The awards are certificates of merit or cash prizes ranging from $10 to $500.

5. According to the above passage, an employee who knows how   5.___
    to do a job in a better way should
        A. be sure it saves enough time to be worthwhile
        B. get paid the money he saves for the city
        C. keep it to himself to avoid being accused of causing
           a speed-up
        D. send his idea to the Employee's Suggestion Program

6. In order to send his idea to the Employee's Suggestion   6.___
   Program, an employee should
       A. ask the Department of Personnel for a special form
       B. get the special form in his own department
       C. mail the idea using Special Delivery
       D. send it on plain, white letter-size paper

7. An employee may send to the Employee's Suggestion Program   7.___
       A. as many ideas as he can think of
       B. no more than one idea each week
       C. no more than ten ideas in a month
       D. only one idea on each part of the job

8. The reason the name of an employee who makes a suggestion   8.___
   is not made known at first is to
       A. give the employee a larger award
       B. help the judges give more awards
       C. insure fairness in judging
       D. only one idea on each part of the job

9. An employee whose suggestion receives an award may be given   9.___
   a
       A. bonus once a year   B. cash prize of up to $500
       C. certificate for $10   D. salary increase of $500

Questions 10-12.

DIRECTIONS: Questions 10 through 12 are to be answered SOLELY on
              the basis of the following passage.

      According to the rules of the Department of Personnel, the work
of every permanent city employee is reviewed and rated by his supervisor at least once a year. The civil service rating system gives
the employee and his supervisor a chance to talk about the progress
made during the past year as well as about those parts of the job
in which the employee needs to do better. In order to receive a pay
increase each year, the employee must have a satisfactory service
rating. Service ratings also count toward an employee's final mark
on a promotion examination.

10. According to the above passage, a permanent city employee   10.___
    is rated AT LEAST once
        A. before his work is reviewed
        B. every six months
        C. yearly by his supervisor
        D. yearly by the Department of Personnel

11. According to the above passage, under the rating system   11.___
    the supervisor and the employee can discuss how
        A. much more work needs to be done next year
        B. the employee did his work last year
        C. the work can be made easier next year
        D. the work of the Department can be increased

3

12. According to the above passage, a permanent city employee   12.___
    will NOT receive a yearly pay increase
    A. if he received a pay increase the year before
    B. if he used his service rating for his mark on a
       promotion examination
    C. if his service rating is unsatisfactory
    D. unless he got some kind of a service rating

Questions 13-16.

DIRECTIONS: Questions 13 through 16 are to be answered SOLELY on
              the basis of the following passage.

    It is an accepted fact that the rank and file employee can fre-
quently advance worthwhile suggestions toward increasing efficiency.
For this reason, an Employees' Suggestion System has been developed
and put into operation. Suitable means have been provided at each
departmental location for the confidential submission of suggestions.
Numerous suggestions have been received thus far and, after study,
about five percent of the ideas submitted are being translated into
action. It is planned to set up, eventually, monetary awards for all
worthwhile suggestions.

13. According to the above passage, a MAJOR reason why an   13.___
    Employees' Suggestion System was established is that
    A. an organized program of improvement is better than a
       haphazard one
    B. employees can often give good suggestions to increase
       efficiency
    C. once a fact is accepted, it is better to act on it than
       to do nothing
    D. the suggestions of rank and file employees were being
       neglected

14. According to the above passage, under the Employees'   14.___
    Suggestion System,
    A. a file of worthwhile suggestions will eventually be
       set up at each departmental location
    B. it is possible for employees to turn in suggestions
       without fellow employees knowing of it
    C. means have been provided for the regular and frequent
       collection of suggestions submitted
    D. provision has been made for the judging of worthwhile
       suggestions by an Employees' Suggestion Committee

15. According to the above passage, it is REASONABLE to assume   15.___
    that
    A. all suggestions must be turned in at a central office
    B. employees who make worthwhile suggestions will be
       promoted
    C. not all the prizes offered will be monetary ones
    D. prizes of money will be given for the best suggestions

16. According to the above passage, of the many suggestions   16.____
    made,
       A. all are first tested
       B. a small part are put into use
       C. most are very worthwhile
       D. samples are studied

Questions 17-20.

DIRECTIONS: Questions 17 through 20 are to be answered SOLELY on
              the basis of the following passage.

      Employees may be granted leaves of absence without pay at the
discretion of the Personnel Officer. Such a leave without pay shall
begin on the first working day on which the employee does not report
for duty and shall continue to the first day on which the employee
returns to duty. The Personnel Division may vary the dates of the
leave for the record so as to conform with payroll periods, but in
no case shall an employee be off the payroll for a different number
of calendar days than would have been the case if the actual dates
mentioned above had been used. An employee who has vacation or
overtime to his credit, which is available for normal use, may take
time off immediately prior to beginning a leave of absence without
pay, chargeable against all or part of such vacation or overtime.

17. According to the above passage, the Personnel Officer must   17.____
       A. decide if a leave of absence without pay should be
          granted
       B. require that a leave end on the last working day of a
          payroll period
       C. see to it that a leave of absence begins on the first
          working day of a pay period
       D. vary the dates of a leave of absence to conform with a
          payroll period

18. According to the above passage, the exact dates of a leave   18.____
    of absence without pay may be varied provided that the
       A. calendar days an employee is off the payroll equal
          the actual leave granted
       B. leave conforms to an even number of payroll periods
       C. leave when granted made provision for variance to
          simplify payroll records
       D. Personnel Officer approves the variation

19. According to the above passage, a leave of absence without   19.____
    pay must extend from the
       A. first day of a calendar period to the first day the
          employee resumes work
       B. first day of a payroll period to the last calendar
          day of the leave
       C. first working day missed to the first day on which
          the employee resumes work
       D. last day on which an employee works through the first
          day he returns to work

5

20. According to the above passage, an employee may take   20.___
    extra time off just before the start of a leave of absence
    without pay if
    A. he charges this extra time against his leave
    B. he has a favorable balance of vacation or overtime
       which has been frozen
    C. the vacation or overtime that he would normally use
       for a leave without pay has not been charged in this
       way before
    D. there is time to his credit which he may use

Question 21.

DIRECTIONS: Question 21 is to be answered SOLELY on the basis of
              the following passage.

    In considering those things which are motivators and incentives
to work, it might be just as erroneous not to give sufficient weight
to money as an incentive as it is to give too much weight. It is not
a problem of establishing a rank-order of importance, but one of
knowing that motivation is a blend or mixture rather than a pure
element. It is simple to say that cultural factors count more than
financial considerations, but this leads only to the conclusion that
our society is financial-oriented.

21. Based on the above passage, in our society, cultural and   21.___
    social motivations to work are
    A. things which cannot be avoided
    B. melded to financial incentives
    C. of less consideration than high pay
    D. not balanced equally with economic or financial con-
       siderations

Question 22.

DIRECTIONS: Question 22 is to be answered SOLELY on the basis of
              the following passage.

    A general principle of training and learning with respect to
people is that they learn more readily if they receive *feedback*.
Essential to maintaining proper motivational levels is knowledge
of results which indicate level of progress. Feedback also assists
the learning process by identifying mistakes. If this kind of
information were not given to the learner, then improper or
inappropriate job performance may be instilled.

22. Based on the above passage, which of the following is MOST   22.___
    accurate?
    A. Learning will not take place without feedback.
    B. In the absence of feedback, improper or inappropriate
       job performance will be learned.
    C. To properly motivate a learner, the learner must have
       his progress made known to him.
    D. Trainees should be told exactly what to do if they are
       to learn properly.

Question 23.

DIRECTIONS: Question 23 is to be answered SOLELY on the basis of
               the following passage.

In a democracy, the obligation of public officials is twofold.
They must not only do an efficient and satisfactory job of administration, but also they must persuade the public that it is an
efficient and satisfactory job. It is a burden which, if properly
assumed, will make democracy work and perpetuate reform government.

23.   The above passage means that   23.____
       A. public officials should try to please everybody
       B. public opinion is instrumental in determining the
          policy of public officials
       C. satisfactory performance of the job of administration
          will eliminate opposition to its work
       D. frank and open procedure in a public agency will aid in
          maintaining progressive government

Question 24.

DIRECTIONS: Question 24 is to be answered SOLELY on the basis of
               the following passage.

Upon retirement for service, a member shall receive a retirement
allowance which shall consist of an annuity which shall be the actuarial equivalent of his accumulated deductions at the time of his
retirement and a pension, in addition to his annuity, which shall be
equal to one service-fraction of his final compensation, multiplied
by the number of years of service since he last became a member
credited to him, and a pension which is the actuarial equivalent of
the reserve-for-increased-take-home-pay to which he may then be
entitled, if any.

24.   According to the above passage, a retirement allowance   24.____
       shall consist of a(n)
       A. annuity, plus a pension, plus an actuarial equivalent
       B. annuity, plus a pension, plus reserve-for-increased-
          take-home-pay, if any
       C. annuity, plus reserve-for-increased-take-home-pay, if
          any, plus final compensation
       D. pension, plus reserve-for-increased-take-home-pay, if
          any, plus accumulated deductions

Question 25.

DIRECTIONS: Question 25 is to be answered SOLELY on the basis of
               the following passage.

Membership in the retirement system shall cease upon the occurrence of any one of the following conditions: when the time out of
service of any member who has total service of less than 25 years,
shall aggregate more than 5 years; when the time out of service of
any member who has total service of 25 years or more, shall aggregate
more than 10 years; when any member shall have withdrawn more than

50% of his accumulated deductions; or when any member shall have withdrawn the cash benefit provided by Section B3-35.0 of the Administrative Code.

25. According to the information in the above passage, member- 25.____
    ship in the retirement system shall cease when an employee
    A. with 17 years of service has been on a leave of absence for 3 years
    B. withdraws 50% of his accumulated deductions
    C. with 28 years of service has been out of service for 10 years
    D. withdraws his cash benefits

————

TEST 2

Questions 1-6.

DIRECTIONS: Questions 1 through 6 are to be answered SOLELY on the basis of the following passage.

Since almost every office has some contact with data-processed records, a stenographer should have some understanding of the basic operations of data processing. Data processing systems now handle about one-third of all office paperwork. On punched cards, magnetic tape, or on other mediums, data are recorded before being fed into the computer for processing. A machine such as the keypunch is used to convert the data written on the source document into the coded symbols on punched cards or tapes. After data has been converted, it must be verified to guarantee absolute accuracy of conversion. In this manner, data becomes a permanent record which can be read by electronic computers that compare, store, compute, and otherwise process data at high speeds.

One key person in a computer installation is a programmer, the man or woman who puts business and scientific problems into special symbolic languages that can be read by the computer. Jobs done by the computer range all the way from payroll operations to chemical process control, but most computer applications are directed toward management data. About half of the programmers employed by business come to their positions with college degrees; the remaining half are promoted to their positions from within the organization on the basis of demonstrated ability without regard to education.

1. Of the following, the BEST title for the above passage is   1.____
   A. THE STENOGRAPHER AS DATA PROCESSOR
   B. THE RELATION OF KEYPUNCHING TO STENOGRAPHY
   C. UNDERSTANDING DATA PROCESSING
   D. PERMANENT OFFICE RECORDS

8

2. According to the above passage, a stenographer should   2.____
   understand the basic operations of data processing because
      A. almost every office today has contact with data
         processed by computer
      B. any office worker may be asked to verify the accuracy
         of data
      C. most offices are involved in the production of
         permanent records
      D. data may be converted into computer language by typing
         on a keypunch

3. According to the above passage, the data which the   3.____
   computer understands is MOST often expressed as
      A. a scientific programming language
      B. records or symbols punched on tape, cards, or other
         mediums
      C. records on cards
      D. records on tape

4. According to the above passage, computers are used MOST   4.____
   often to handle
      A. management data
      B. problems of higher education
      C. the control of chemical processes
      D. payroll operations

5. Computer programming is taught in many colleges and   5.____
   business schools.
   The above passage IMPLIES that programmers in industry
      A. must have professional training
      B. need professional training to advance
      C. must have at least a college education to do adequate
         programming tasks
      D. do not need college education to do programming work

6. According to the above passage, data to be processed by   6.____
   computer should be
      A. recent   B. complete   C. basic   D. verified

Questions 7-10.

DIRECTIONS: Questions 7 through 10 are to be answered SOLELY on
              the basis of the following passage.

There is nothing that will take the place of good sense on the
part of the stenographer. You may be perfect in transcribing exactly
what the dictator says and your speed may be adequate, but without an
understanding of the dictator's intent as well as his words, you are
likely to be a mediocre secretary.

A serious error that is made when taking dictation is putting
down something that does not make sense. Most people who dictate
material would rather be asked to repeat and explain than to receive
transcribed material which has errors due to inattention or doubt.
Many dictators request that their grammar be corrected by their
secretaries, but unless specifically asked to do so, secretaries

should not do it without first checking with the dictator. Secretaries should be aware that, in some cases, dictators may use incorrect grammar or slang expressions to create a particular effect.

Some people dictate commas, periods, and paragraphs, while others expect the stenographer to know when, where, and how to punctuate. A well-trained secretary should be able to indicate the proper punctuation by listening to the pauses and tones of the dictator's voice.

A stenographer who has taken dictation from the same person for a period of time should be able to understand him under most conditions. By increasing her tact, alertness, and efficiency, a secretary can become more competent.

7. According to the above passage, which of the following   7.___
   statements concerning the dictation of punctuation is
   CORRECT?
   A
       A. dictator may use incorrect punctuation to create a
          desired style
       B. dictator should indicate all punctuation
       C. stenographer should know how to punctuate based on
          the pauses and tones of the dictator
       D. stenographer should not type any punctuation if it
          has not been dictated to her

8. According to the above passage, how should secretaries   8.___
   handle grammatical errors in a dictation?
   Secretaries should
       A. *not correct* grammatical errors unless the dictator
          is aware that this is being done
       B. *correct* grammatical errors by having the dictator
          repeat the line with proper pauses
       C. *correct* grammatical errors if they have checked the
          correctness in a grammar book
       D. *correct* grammatical errors based on their own good
          sense

9. If a stenographer is confused about the method of spacing   9.___
   and indenting of a report which has just been dictated to
   her, she GENERALLY should
       A. do the best she can
       B. ask the dictator to explain what she should do
       C. try to improve her ability to understand dictated
          material
       D. accept the fact that her stenographic ability is not
          adequate

10. In the last line of the first paragraph, the word *mediocre* 10.___
    means MOST NEARLY
        A. superior   B. disregarded
        C. respected   D. second-rate

Questions 11-12.

DIRECTIONS: Questions 11 and 12 are to be answered SOLELY on the
basis of the following passage.

The number of legible carbon copies required to be produced determines the weight of the carbon paper to be used. When only one copy
is made, heavy carbon paper is satisfactory. Most typists, however,
use medium-weight carbon paper and find it serviceable for up to three
or four copies. If five or more copies are to be made, it is wise to
use light carbon paper. On the other hand, the finish of carbon paper
to be used depends largely on the stroke of the typist and, in lesser
degree, on the number of copies to be made and on whether the typewriter has pica or elite type. A soft-finish carbon paper should be
used if the typist's touch is light or if a noiseless machine is used.
It is desirable for the average typist to use medium-finish carbon
paper for ordinary work, when only a few carbon copies are required.
Elite type requires a harder carbon finish than pica type for the
same number of copies.

11. According to the above passage, the lighter the carbon   11.____
    paper used,
    A. the softer the finish of the carbon paper will be
    B. the greater the number of legible carbon copies that
       can be made
    C. the greater the number of times the carbon paper can
       be used
    D. the lighter the typist's touch should be

12. According to the above passage, the MOST important factor   12.____
    which determines whether the finish of carbon paper to be
    used in typing should be hard, medium, or soft is
    A. the touch of the typist
    B. the number of carbon copies required
    C. whether the type in the typewriter is pica or elite
    D. whether a machine with pica type will produce the same
       number of carbon copies as a machine with elite type

Questions 13-16.

DIRECTIONS: Questions 13 through 16 are to be answered SOLELY on
the basis of the following passage.

Modern office methods, geared to ever higher speeds and aimed at
ever greater efficiency, are largely the result of the typewriter. The
typewriter is a substitute for handwriting and, in the hands of a
skilled typist, not only turns out letters and other documents at
least three times faster than a penman can do the work, but turns out
the greater volume more uniformly and legibly. With the use of carbon
paper and onionskin paper, identical copies can be made at the same
time.

The typewriter, besides its effect on the conduct of business and
government, has had a very important effect on the position of women.
The typewriter has done much to bring women into business and government, and today there are vastly more women than men typists. Many

women have used the keys of the typewriter to climb the ladder to responsible managerial positions.

The typewriter, as its name implies, employs type to make an ink impression on paper. For many years, the manual typewriter was the standard machine used. Today, the electric typewriter is dominant, and completely automatic electronic typewriters are coming into wider use.

The mechanism of the office manual typewriter includes a set of keys arranged systematically in rows; a semicircular frame of type, connected to the keys by levers; the carriage, or paper carrier; a rubber roller, called a platen, against which the type strikes; and an inked ribbon which make the impression of the type character when the key strikes it.

13. The above passage mentions a number of good features of the combination of a skilled typist and a typewriter. 13.____
    Of the following, the feature which is NOT mentioned in the passage is
    A. speed   B. uniformity
    C. reliability   D. legibility

14. According to the above passage, a skilled typist can 14.____
    A. turn out at least five carbon copies of typed matter
    B. type at least three times faster than a penman can write
    C. type more than 80 words a minute
    D. readily move into a managerial position

15. According to the above passage, which of the following is NOT part of the mechanism of a manual typewriter? 15.____
    A. Carbon paper   B. Paper carrier
    C. Platen   D. Inked ribbon

16. According to the above passage, the typewriter has helped 16.____
    A. men more than women in business
    B. women in career advancement into management
    C. men and women equally, but women have taken better advantage of it
    D. more women than men, because men generally dislike routine typing work

Questions 17-21.

DIRECTIONS: Questions 17 through 21 are to be answered SOLELY on the basis of the following passage.

The recipient gains an impression of a typewritten letter before he begins to read the message. Factors which provide for a good first impression include margins and spacing that are visually pleasing, formal parts of the letter which are correctly placed according to the style of the letter, copy which is free of obvious erasures and over-strikes, and transcript that is even and clear. The problem for the typist is that of how to produce that first, positive impression of her work.

There are several general rules which a typist can follow when she wishes to prepare a properly spaced letter on a sheet of letter-head. Ordinarily, the width of a letter should not be less than four inches nor more than six inches. The side margins should also have a desirable relation to the bottom margin and the space between the letterhead and the body of the letter. Usually the most appealing arrangement is when the side margins are even and the bottom margin is slightly wider than the side margins. In some offices, however, standard line length is used for all business letters, and the secretary then varies the spacing between the date line and the inside address according to the length of the letter.

17. The BEST title for the above passage would be   17.____
    A. WRITING OFFICE LETTERS
    B. MAKING GOOD FIRST IMPRESSIONS
    C. JUDGING WELL-TYPED LETTERS
    D. GOOD PLACING AND SPACING FOR OFFICE LETTERS

18. According to the above passage, which of the following   18.____
might be considered the way in which people very quickly
judge the quality of work which has been typed?
By
    A. measuring the margins to see if they are correct
    B. looking at the spacing and cleanliness of the typescript
    C. scanning the body of the letter for meaning
    D. reading the date line and address for errors

19. What, according to the above passage, would be definitely   19.____
UNDESIRABLE as the average line length of a typed letter?
    A. 4"   B. 5"   C. 6"   D. 7"

20. According to the above passage, when the line length is   20.____
kept standard, the secretary
    A. does not have to vary the spacing at all since this
       also is standard
    B. adjusts the spacing between the date line and inside
       address for different lengths of letters
    C. uses the longest line as a guideline for spacing between
       the date line and inside address
    D. varies the number of spaces between the lines

21. According to the above passage, side margins are MOST   21.____
pleasing when they
    A. are even and somewhat smaller than the bottom margin
    B. are slightly wider than the bottom margin
    C. vary with the length of the letter
    D. are figured independently from the letterhead and the
      body of the letter

Questions 22-25.

DIRECTIONS: Questions 22 through 25 are to be answered SOLELY on
the basis of the following passage.

Typed pages can reflect the simplicity of modern art in a
machine age. Lightness and evenness can be achieved by proper

layout and balance of typed lines and white space. Instead of solid, cramped masses of uneven, crowded typing, there should be a pleasing balance up and down as well as horizontal.

To have real balance, your page must have a center. The eyes see the center of the sheet slightly above the real center. This is the way both you and the reader see it. Try imagining a line down the center of the page that divides the paper in equal halves. On either side of your paper, white space and blocks of typing need to be similar in size and shape. Although left and right margins should be equal, top and bottom margins need not be as exact. It looks better to hold a bottom border wider than a top margin, so that your typing rests upon a cushion of white space. To add interest to the appearance of the page, try making one paragraph between one-half and two-thirds the size of an adjacent paragraph.

Thus, by taking full advantage of your typewriter, the pages that you type will not only be accurate but will also be attractive.

22. It can be inferred from the above passage that the BASIC importance of proper balancing on a typed page is that proper balancing   22.___
    A. makes a typed page a work of modern art
    B. provides exercise in proper positioning of a typewriter
    C. increases the amount of typed copy on the paper
    D. draws greater attention and interest to the page

23. A reader will tend to see the center of a typed page   23.___
    A. somewhat higher than the true center
    B. somewhat lower than the true center
    C. on either side of the true center
    D. about two-thirds of an inch above the true center

24. Which of the following suggestions is NOT given by the above passage?   24.___
    A. Bottom margins may be wider than top borders.
    B. Keep all paragraphs approximately the same size.
    C. Divide your page with an imaginary line down the middle.
    D. Side margins should be equalized.

25. Of the following, the BEST title for the above passage is   25.___
    A. INCREASING THE ACCURACY OF THE TYPED PAGE
    B. DETERMINATION OF MARGINS FOR TYPED COPY
    C. LAYOUT AND BALANCE OF THE TYPED PAGE
    D. HOW TO TAKE FULL ADVANTAGE OF THE TYPEWRITER

TEST 3

Questions 1-5.

DIRECTIONS: Questions 1 through 5 are to be answered SOLELY on the basis of the following passage.

A written report is a communication of information from one person to another. It is an account of some matter especially investigated, however routine that matter may be. The ultimate basis of any good written report is facts, which become known through observation and verification. Good written reports may seem to be no more than general ideas and opinions. However, in such cases, the facts leading to these opinions were gathered, verified, and reported earlier, and the opinions are dependent upon these facts. Good style, proper form, and emphasis cannot make a good written report out of unreliable information and bad judgment; but on the other hand, solid investigation and brilliant thinking are not likely to become very useful until they are effectively communicated to others. If a person's work calls for written reports, then his work is often no better than his written reports.

1. Based on the information in the above passage, it can be concluded that opinions expressed in a report should be
    A. based on facts which are gathered and reported
    B. emphasized repeatedly when they result from a special investigation
    C. kept to a minimum
    D. separated from the body of the report

1.____

2. In the above passage, the one of the following which is mentioned as a way of establishing facts is
    A. authority   B. communication
    C. reporting   D. verification

2.____

3. According to the above passage, the characteristic shared by ALL written reports is that they are
    A. accounts of routine matters
    B. transmissions of information
    C. reliable and logical
    D. written in proper form

3.____

4. Which of the following conclusions can LOGICALLY be drawn from the information given in the above passage?
    A. Brilliant thinking can make up for unreliable information in a report.
    B. One method of judging an individual's work is the quality of the written reports he is required to submit.
    C. Proper form and emphasis can make a good report out of unreliable information.
    D. Good written reports that seem to be no more than general ideas should be rewritten.

4.____

5. Which of the following suggested titles would be MOST   5.____
    appropriate for the above passage?
        A. GATHERING AND ORGANIZING FACTS
        B. TECHNIQUES OF OBSERVATION
        C. NATURE AND PURPOSE OF REPORTS
        D. REPORTS AND OPINIONS: DIFFERENCES AND SIMILARITIES

Questions 6-8.

DIRECTIONS: Questions 6 through 8 are to be answered SOLELY on
               the basis of the following passage.

    The most important unit of the mimeograph machine is a perforated
metal drum over which is stretched a cloth ink pad. A reservoir inside the drum contains the ink which flows through the perforations
and saturates the ink pad. To operate the machine, the operator first
removes from the machine the protective sheet, which keeps the ink
from drying while the machine is not in use. He then hooks the stencil face down on the drum, draws the stencil smoothly over the drum,
and fastens the stencil at the bottom. The speed with which the drum
turns determines the blackness of the copies printed. Slow turning
gives heavy, black copies; fast turning gives light, clear-cut reproductions. If reproductions are run on other than porous paper, slip-
sheeting is necessary to prevent smearing. Often, the printed copy
fails to drop readily as it comes from the machine. This may be due
to static electricity. To remedy this difficulty, the operator
fastens a strip of tinsel from side to side near the impression roller
so that the printed copy just touches the soft stems of the tinsel
as it is ejected from the machine, thus grounding the static electricity to the frame of the machine.

6. According to the above passage,   6.____
        A. turning the drum fast produces light copies
        B. stencils should be placed face up on the drum
        C. ink pads should be changed daily
        D. slip-sheeting is necessary when porous paper is being
           used

7. According to the above passage, when a mimeograph machine   7.____
    is not in use,
        A. the ink should be drained from the drum
        B. the ink pad should be removed
        C. the machine should be covered with a protective sheet
        D. the counter should be set at zero

8. According to the above passage, static electricity is   8.____
    grounded to the frame of the mimeograph machine by means of
        A. a slip-sheeting device
        B. a strip of tinsel
        C. an impression roller
        D. hooks located at the top of the drum

Questions 9-10.

DIRECTIONS: Questions 9 and 10 are to be answered SOLELY on the basis of the following passage.

The proofreading of material typed from copy is performed more accurately and more speedily when two persons perform this work as a team. The person who did not do the typing should read aloud the original copy while the person who did the typing should check the reading against the typed copy. The reader should speak very slowly and repeat the figures, using a different grouping of numbers when repeating the figures. For example, in reading 1967, the reader may say *one-nine-six-seven* on first reading the figure and *nineteen-sixty-seven* on repeating the figure. The reader should read all punctuation marks, taking nothing for granted. Since mistakes can occur anywhere, everything typed should be proofread. To avoid confusion, the proofreading team should use the standard proofreading marks, which are given in most dictionaries.

9. According to the above passage, the   9.___
    A. person who holds the typed copy is called the reader
    B. two members of a proofreading team should take turns
       in reading the typed copy aloud
    C. typed copy should be checked by the person who did the
       typing
    D. person who did not do the typing should read aloud
       from the typed copy

10. According to the above passage,   10.___
    A. it is unnecessary to read the period at the end of a
       sentence
    B. typographical errors should be noted on the original
       copy
    C. each person should develop his own set of proofreading
       marks
    D. figures should be read twice

Questions 11-16.

DIRECTIONS: Questions 11 through 16 are to be answered SOLELY on the basis of the above passage.

Basic to every office is the need for proper lighting. Inadequate lighting is a familiar cause of fatigue and serves to create a somewhat dismal atmosphere in the office. One requirement of proper lighting is that it be of an appropriate intensity. Intensity is measured in foot candles. According to the Illuminating Engineering Society of New York, for casual seeing tasks such as in reception rooms, inactive file rooms, and other service areas, it is recommended that the amount of light be 30 foot-candles. For ordinary seeing tasks such as reading, work in active file rooms, and in mailrooms, the recommended lighting is 100 foot-candles. For very difficult seeing tasks such as accounting, transcribing, and business machine use, the recommended lighting is 150 foot-candles.

Lighting intensity is only one requirement. Shadows and glare are to be avoided. For example, the larger the proportion of a ceiling filled with lighting units, the more glare-free and comfortable the lighting will be. Natural lighting from windows is not too dependable because on dark wintry days, windows yield little usable light, and on sunny summer afternoons, the glare from windows may be very distracting. Desks should not face the windows. Finally, the main lighting source ought to be overhead and to the left of the user.

11. According to the above passage, insufficient light in the office may cause   11.____
  A. glare   B. shadows
  C. tiredness   D. distraction

12. Based on the above passage, which of the following must be considered when planning lighting arrangements? 12.____
The
  A. amount of natural light present
  B. amount of work to be done
  C. level of difficulty of work to be done
  D. type of activity to be carried out

13. It can be inferred from the above passage that a well-coordinated lighting scheme is LIKELY to result in 13.____
  A. greater employee productivity
  B. elimination of light reflection
  C. lower lighting cost
  D. more use of natural light

14. Of the following, the BEST title for the above passage is 14.____
  A. CHARACTERISTICS OF LIGHT
  B. LIGHT MEASUREMENT DEVICES
  C. FACTORS TO CONSIDER WHEN PLANNING LIGHTING SYSTEMS
  D. COMFORT VS. COST WHEN DEVISING LIGHTING ARRANGEMENTS

15. According to the above passage, a foot-candle is a measurement of the 15.____
  A. number of bulbs used
  B. strength of the light
  C. contrast between glare and shadow
  D. proportion of the ceiling filled with lighting units

16. According to the above passage, the number of foot-candles of light that would be needed to copy figures onto a payroll is ____ foot-candles. 16.____
  A. less than 30   B. 30
  C. 100   D. 150

Questions 17-23.

DIRECTIONS: Questions 17 through 23 are to be answered SOLELY on the basis of the following passage, which is the Fee Schedule of a hypothetical college.

FEE SCHEDULE

A. A candidate for any baccalaureate degree is not required to pay tuition fees for undergraduate courses until he exceeds 128 credits. Candidates exceeding 128 credits in undergraduate courses are charged at the rate of $100 a credit for each credit of undergraduate course work in excess of 128. Candidates for a baccalaureate degree who are taking graduate courses must pay the same fee as any other student taking graduate courses.

B. Non-degree students and college graduates are charged tuition fees for courses, whether undergraduate or graduate, at the rate of $180 a credit. For such students, there is an additional charge of $150 for each class hour per week in excess of the number of course credits. For example, if a three-credit course meets five hours a week, there is an additional charge for the extra two hours. Graduate courses are shown with a (G) before the course number.

C. All students are required to pay the laboratory fees indicated after the number of credits given for that course.

D. All students must pay a $250 general fee each semester.

E. Candidates for a baccalaureate degree are charged a $150 medical insurance fee for each semester. All other students are charged a $100 medical insurance fee each semester.

17. Miss Burton is not a candidate for a degree. She registers 17.___
    for the following courses in the spring semester: Economics 12, 4 hours a week, 3 credits; History(G)23, 4 hours a week, 3 credits; English 1, 2 hours a week, 2 credits.
    The TOTAL amount in fees that Miss Burton must pay is
    A. less than $2000
    B. at least $2000 but less than $2100
    C. at least $2100 but less than $2200
    D. $2200 or over

18. Miss Gray is not a candidate for a degree. She registers   18.___
    for the following courses in the fall semester: History 3, 3 hours a week, 3 credits; English 5, 3 hours a week, 2 credits; Physics 5, 6 hours a week, 3 credits, laboratory fee $60; Mathematics 7, 4 hours a week, 3 credits.
    The TOTAL amount in fees that Miss Gray must pay is
    A. less than $3150
    B. at least $3150 but less than $3250
    C. at least $3250 but less than $3350
    D. $3350 or over

19. Mr. Wall is a candidate for the Bachelor of Arts degree   19.____
    and has completed 126 credits. He registers for the
    following courses in the spring semester, his final
    semester at college: French 4, 3 hours a week, 3 credits;
    Physics (G) 15, 6 hours a week, 3 credits, laboratory fee
    $80; History (G) 33, 4 hours a week, 3 credits.
    The TOTAL amount in fees that this candidate must pay is
       A. less than $2100
       B. at least $2100 but less than $2300
       C. at least $2300 but less than $2500
       D. $2500

20. Mr. Tindall, a candidate for the B.A. degree, has com-   20.____
    pleted 122 credits of undergraduate courses. He registers
    for the following courses in his final semester: English
    31, 3 hours a week, 3 credits; Philosophy 12, 4 hours a
    week, 4 credits; Anthropology 15, 3 hours a week, 3 credits;
    Economics (G) 68, 3 hours a week, 3 credits.
    The TOTAL amount in fees that Mr. Tindall must pay in his
    final semester is
       A. less than $1200
       B. at least $1200 but less than $1400
       C. at least $1400 but less than $1600
       D. $1600

21. Mr. Cantrell, who was graduated from the college a year   21.____
    ago, registers for graduate courses in the fall semester.
    Each course for which he registers carries the same number
    of credits as the number of hours a week it meets.
    If he pays a total of $1530, including a $100 laboratory fee,
    the number of credits for which he is registered is
       A. 4   B. 5   C. 6   D. 7

22. Miss Jayson, who is not a candidate for a degree, has   22.____
    registered for several courses including a lecture course
    in History. She withdraws from the course in History for
    which she had paid the required course fee of $690.
    The number of hours that this course is scheduled to meet is
       A. 4   B. 5   C. 2   D. 3

23. Mr. Van Arsdale, a graduate of a college is Iowa, registers 23.____
    for the following courses in one semester: Chemistry 35,
    5 hours a week, 3 credits; Biology 13, 4 hours a week, 3
    credits, laboratory fee $150; Mathematics (G) 179, 3 hours
    a week, 3 credits.
    The TOTAL amount in fees that Mr. Van Arsdale must pay is
       A. less than $2400
       B. at least $2400 but less than $2500
       C. at least $2500 but less than $2600
       D. at least $2600 or over

Questions 24-25.

DIRECTIONS: Questions 24 and 25 are to be answered SOLELY on the basis of the following passage.

A duplex envelope is an envelope composed of two sections securely fastened together so that they become one mailing piece. This type of envelope makes it possible for a first class letter to be delivered simultaneously with third or fourth class matter and yet not require payment of the much higher first class postage rate on the entire mailing. First class postage is paid only on the letter which goes in the small compartment, third or fourth class postage being paid on the contents of the larger compartment. The larger compartment generally has an ungummed flap or clasp for sealing. The first class or smaller compartment has a gummed flap for sealing. Postal regulations require that the exact amount of postage applicable to each compartment be separately attached to it.

24. On the basis of the above passage, it is MOST accurate to   24.___
    state that
    A. the smaller compartment is placed inside the larger
       compartment before mailing
    B. the two compartments may be detached and mailed
       separately
    C. two classes of mailing matter may be mailed as a unit
       at two different postage rates
    D. the more expensive postage rate is paid on the matter
       in the larger compartment

25. When a duplex envelope is used, the   25.___
    A. first class compartment may be sealed with a clasp
    B. correct amount of postage must be placed on each
       compartment
    C. compartment containing third or fourth class mail
       requires a gummed flap for sealing
    D. full amount of postage for both compartments may be
       placed on the larger compartment

———

21

KEY (CORRECT ANSWERS)

TEST 1	TEST 2	TEST 3
1. B	1. C	1. A
2. A	2. A	2. D
3. C	3. B	3. B
4. A	4. A	4. B
5. D	5. D	5. C
6. B	6. D	6. A
7. A	7. C	7. C
8. C	8. A	8. B
9. B	9. B	9. C
10. C	10. D	10. D
11. B	11. B	11. C
12. C	12. A	12. D
13. B	13. C	13. A
14. B	14. B	14. C
15. D	15. A	15. B
16. B	16. B	16. D
17. A	17. D	17. B
18. A	18. B	18. A
19. C	19. D	19. B
20. D	20. B	20. B
21. B	21. A	21. C
22. C	22. D	22. A
23. D	23. A	23. C
24. B	24. B	24. C
25. D	25. C	25. B

DOCUMENTS AND FORMS
PREPARING WRITTEN MATERIALS
EXAMINATION SECTION

DIRECTIONS FOR THIS SECTION:
Each question or incomplete statement is followed by several suggested answers or completions. Select the one that BEST answers the
question or completes the statement. *PRINT THE LETTER OF THE CORRECT
ANSWER IN THE SPACE AT THE RIGHT.*

TEST 1

1. The office layout chart is a sketch of the physical ar-   1. ...
   rangement of the office to which has been added the flow
   lines of the principal work performed there.
   Which one of the following states the BEST advantage of
   superimposing the work flow onto the desk layout?
   A. Lighting and acoustics can be improved.
   B. Line and staff relationships can be determined.
   C. Obvious misarrangements can be corrected.
   D. The number of delays can be determined.
2. An advantage of the multiple process chart over the flow   2. ...
   process chart is that the multiple process chart shows the
   A. individual worker's activity   B. number of delays
   C. sequence of operations
   D. simultaneous flow of work in several departments
3. Of the following, which is the MAJOR advantage of a micro-   3. ...
   film record retention system?
   A. Filing can follow the terminal digit system.
   B. Retrieving documents from the files is faster.
   C. Significant space is saved in storing records.
   D. To read a microfilm record, a film reader is not
      necessary.
4. Assume that you are in the process of eliminating unneces-   4. ...
   sary forms.
   The answer to which one of the following questions would
   be LEAST relevant?
   A. Could the information be obtained elsewhere?
   B. Is the form properly designed?
   C. Is the form used as intended?
   D. Is the purpose of the form essential to the operation?
5. Use of color in forms adds to their cost. Sometimes, how-   5. ...
   ever, the use of color will greatly simplify procedure and
   more than pay for itself in time saved and errors eliminated.
   This is ESPECIALLY true when
   A. a form passes through many reviewers
   B. considerable sorting is required
   C. the form is other than a standard size
   D. the form will not be sent through the mail
6. Of the following techniques, the one *generally* employed   6. ...
   and considered BEST in forms design is to provide writing
   lines into boxes with captions printed in small type
   A. centered in the lower part of the box
   B. centered in the upper part of the box
   C. in the upper left-hand corner of the box
   D. in the lower right-hand corner of the box
7. Many forms authorities advocate the construction of a func-   7. ...
   tional forms file or index.
   If such a file is set up, the MOST effective way of classify-
   ing forms for such an index is classification by

A. department
B. form number
C. name or type of form
D. subject to which the form applies

8. Of the following, the symbol
as used in a systems flow
chart denotes
A. decision
B. document
C. manual operation
D. process

8. ...

9. Assume you are assigned to analyze the details of the
procedures a clerk follows in order to complete filling out
an invoice or a requisition. Your purpose is to simplify
and shorten the procedure he has been trained to use.
The BEST appropriate chart for this purpose would be the
A. block flow diagram   B. flow process chart
C. forms flow chart   D. work distribution chart

9. ...

10. What *generally* is the PRINCIPAL objection to the use of
form letters? The
A. difficulty of developing a form letter to serve the
purpose
B. excessive time involved in selecting the proper form
letter
C. errors in selecting form letters
D. impersonality of form letters

10. ...

11. In process charting, the symbol which is used when conditions (except those which intentionally change the physical or chemical characteristics of the object) do not permit or require immediate performance, is

A.   B.   C.   D.

11. ...

12. Assume that you are making a study of a central headquarters office which processes claims received from a
number of district offices. You notice the following
problems: Some employees are usually busy, while others
doing the same kind of work in the same grade have little
to do; high level professional people frequently spend
considerable time searching for files in the file room.
Which of the following charts would be MOST useful to
record and analyze the data needed to help solve these
problems?
A. Forms distribution chart B. Process chart
C. Space layout chart   D. Work distribution chart

12. ...

13. Which of the following questions has the LEAST significant bearing on the analysis of the paperwork flow?
A. How is the work brought into the department and how
is it taken away?
B. How many work stations are involved in processing
the work within the department?
C. Is the work received and removed in the proper
quantity?
D. Where is the supervisor's desk located in relationship to those he supervises?

13. ...

2

14. Which of the following does NOT have significant bearing   14. ...
    on the arrangement, sequence, and zoning of information
    into box captions? The
       A. layout of the source documents from which the infor-
          mation is taken
       B. logical flow of data
       C. needs of forms to be prepared from this form
       D. type of print to be employed
15. In determining the space requirements of a form and the   15. ...
    size of the boxes to be used, PRIMARY consideration should
    be given to the
       A. distribution of the form
       B. method of entry, i.e., handwritten or machine,and
          type of machine
       C. number of copies   D. number of items to be entered
16. Of the following, the BEST technique to follow when pro-   16. ...
    viding instructions for the completion and routing of a
    form is to
       A. imprint the instructions on the face of the form
       B. imprint the instructions on the back of the form
       C. provide a written procedure to accompany the form
       D. provide verbal instructions when issuing the form
17. A forms layout style where a separate space in the shape   17. ...
    of a box is provided for each item of information requested
    and the caption or question for each item is shown in the
    upper left-hand corner of each box, is known as the
       A. box style   B. check box style
       C. check list style D. check box and check list style
18. The BEST type of chart to use in showing the absolute   18. ...
    movement or change of a continuous series of data over a
    period of time, such as changes in prices, employment or
    expenses, is usually a
       A. bar chart   B. line chart
       C. multiple bar chart D. pie chart
19. In order to secure information on several specific points   19. ...
    from all the tenants of a project, it has been suggested
    that a questionnaire be distributed to be completed and
    returned by the tenants.
    The use of such a procedure is, generally,
       A. desirable, because it is a valuable means of building
          the cooperative relationship which should exist between
          tenants and management
       B. desirable, because it provides a written record of each
          tenant's reply
       C. undesirable, because distribution and collection of
          questionnaires is time-consuming
       D. undesirable, because it makes no provision for the ex-
          pression of related information or viewpoints
20. A functional forms file is a collection of forms which   20. ...
    are grouped by
       A. purpose   B. department   C. title   D. subject
21. All of the following are reasons to consult a records   21. ...
    retention schedule EXCEPT one. Which one is that? To
    determine
       A. whether something should be filed
       B. how long something should stay in file

3

    C. who should be assigned to filing
    D. when something on file should be destroyed

22. Listed below are four of the steps in the process of pre- 22. ...
paring correspondence for filing. If they were to be put
in logical sequence, the SECOND step would be
    A. preparing cross-reference sheets or cards
    B. coding the correspondence using a classification system
    C. sorting the correspondence in the order to be filed
    D. checking for follow-up action required and preparing a
       follow-up slip

23. New material added to a file folder should *usually* be 23. ...
inserted
    A. in the order of importance (the most important in front)
    B. in the order of importance (the most important in back)
    C. chronologically (most recent in front)
    D. chronologically (most recent in back)

24. An individual is looking for a name in the white pages 24. ...
of a telephone directory.
Which of the following BEST describes the system of filing
found there? A(n)
    A. alphabetic file   B. sequential file
    C. locator file   D. index file

25. The MAIN purpose of a tickler file is to 25. ...
    A. help prevent overlooking matters that require future
       attention
    B. check on adequacy of past performance
    C. pinpoint responsibility for recurring daily tasks
    D. reduce the volume of material kept in general files

TEST 2

1. A *good* record-keeping system includes all of the following 1. ...
procedures EXCEPT the
    A. filing of useless records
    B. destruction of certain files
    C. transferring of records from one type of file to
       another
    D. creation of inactive files

2. A new program is being set up for which certain new forms 2. ...
will be needed. You have been asked to design these forms.
Of the following, the FIRST step you should take in planning
the forms is
    A. finding out the exact purpose for which each form will
       be used
    B. deciding what size of paper should be used for each form
    C. determining whether multiple copies will be needed for
       any of the forms
    D. setting up a new filing system to handle the new forms

3. Assume that your department is being moved to new and 3. ...
larger quarters, and that you have been asked to suggest
an office layout for the central clerical office.
Of the following, your FIRST step in planning the new layout should *ordinarily* be to
    A. find out how much money has been budgeted for furniture
       and equipment

4

    B. make out work-flow and traffic-flow charts for the
        clerical operations
    C. measure each piece of furniture and equipment that
        is presently in use
    D. determine which files should be moved to a storage
        area or destroyed

4. In modern office layouts, screens and dividers are often   4. ...
    used instead of walls to set off working groups. Advan-
    tages given for this approach have included *all* of the
    following EXCEPT
    A. more frequent communication between different working
        groups
    B. reduction in general noise level
    C. fewer objections from employees who are transferred
        to different groups
    D. cost savings from increased sharing of office equipment

5. Of the following, the CHIEF reason for moving less active   5. ...
    material from active to inactive files is to
    A. dispose of material that no longer has any use
    B. keep the active files down to a manageable size
    C. make sure that no material over a year old remains in
        active files
    D. separate temporary records from permanent records

6. On a general organization chart, staff positions NORMALLY   6. ...
    should be pictured
    A. directly above the line positions to which they report
    B. to the sides of the main flow lines
    C. within the box of the highest level subordinate posi-
        tions pictured
    D. directly below the line positions which report to them

7. When an administrator is diagramming an office layout, of   7. ...
    the following, his PRIMARY job, *generally*, should be to
    indicate the
    A. lighting intensities that will be required by each
        operation
    B. noise level that will be produced by the various
        equipment employed in the office
    C. direction of the work flow and the distance involved
        in each transfer
    D. durability of major pieces of office equipment cur-
        rently in use or to be utilized

8. One common guideline or rule-of-thumb ratio for evaluating   8. ...
    the efficiency of files is the number of records requested
    divided by the number of records filed.
    Generally, if this ratio is very low, it would point MOST
    directly to the need for
    A. improving the indexing and coding system
    B. improving the charge-out procedures
    C. exploring the need for transferring records from ac-
        tive storage to the archives
    D. exploring the need to encourage employees to keep more
        records in their private files

9. The GREATEST percentage of money spent on preparing and   9. ...
    keeping the usual records in an office, *generally*, is
    expended for which one of the following?
    A. Renting space in which to place the record-keeping
        equipment

  B. Paying salaries of record-preparing and record-keep-
     ing personnel
  C. Depreciation of purchased record-preparation and
     record-keeping equipment
  D. Paper and forms upon which to place the records
10. The MAXIMUM number of 2 3/4" x 4 1/4" size forms which   10. ...
    may be obtained from two reams of 17" x 22" paper is
     A. 4,000   B. 8,000   C. 16,000   D. 32,000
11. Manually-operated typewriters MOST generally tend to   11. ...
    have which one of the following advantages, as compared
    with electric typewriters?
     A. Lower maintenance costs   B. Higher quality copy
     C. Greater output with less energy being expended
     D. Greater number of legible copies per typing
12. Generally, the actual floor space occupied by a standard   12. ...
    letter-size office file cabinet, when closed, is, *most
    nearly,*
     A. 1/2 square foot   B. 3 square feet
     C. 7 square feet   D. 11 square feet
13. In general, the CHIEF economy of using multicopy forms   13. ...
    is in
     A. the paper on which the form is printed
     B. printing the form   C. employee time
     D. carbon paper
14. Suppose your supervisor has asked you to develop a form   14. ...
    to record certain information needed. The FIRST thing
    you should do is to
     A. determine the type of data that will be recorded
        repeatedly, so that it can be preprinted
     B. study the relationship of the form to the job to be
        accomplished, so that the form can be planned
     C. determine the information that will be recorded in
        the same place on each copy of the form, so that it
        can be used as a check
     D. find out who will be responsible for supplying the
        information so that space can be provided for their
        signatures
15. Of the following, which is usually the MOST important   15. ...
    guideline in writing business letters? A letter should be
     A. neat   B. written in a formalized style
     C. written in clear language intelligible to the reader
     D. written in the past tense
16. Suppose you are asked to edit a policy statement. You   16. ...
    note that personal pronouns like "you," "we," and "I"
    are used freely.
    Which of the following statements BEST applies to this use
    of personal pronouns? It
     A. is proper usage because written business language should
        not be different from carefully spoken business language
     B. requires correction because it is ungrammatical
     C. is proper because it is clearer and has a warmer tone
     D. requires correction because policies should be expressed
        in an impersonal manner
17. Good business letters are coherent. To be *coherent* means   17. ...
    to
     A. keep only one unifying idea in the message

    B. present the total message
    C. use simple, direct words for the message
    D. tie together the various ideas in the message

18. Proper division of a letter into paragraphs requires that   18. ...
the writer of business letters should, as much as possible,
be sure that
    A. each paragraph is short
    B. each paragraph develops discussion of just one topic
    C. each paragraph repeats the theme of the total message
    D. there are at least two paragraphs for every message

19. An editor is given a letter with this initial paragraph: 19. ...
"We have received your letter, which we read with interest,
and we are happy to respond to your question. In fact, we
talked with several people in our office to get ideas to
send to you."
Which of the following is it MOST reasonable for the editor
to conclude? The paragraph is
    A. concise   B. communicating something of value
    C. unnecessary D. coherent

20. Suppose that one of your duties is to dictate responses   20. ...
to routine requests from the public for information. A
letter writer asks for information which, as expressed in
a one-sentence, explicit agency rule, cannot be given out
to the public.
Of the following ways of answering the letter, which is
the MOST efficient?
    A. Quote verbatim that section of the agency rules which
       prohibits giving this information to the public
    B. Without quoting the rule, explain why you cannot ac-
       cede to the request and suggest alternative sources
    C. Describe how carefully the request was considered be-
       fore classifying it as subject to the rule forbidding
       the issuance of such information
    D. Acknowledge receipt of the letter and advise that the
       requested information is not released to the public

21. Suppose you have been asked to write and to prepare for   21. ...
reproduction new departmental vacation leave regulations.
After you have written the new regulations, all of which
fit on one page, which one of the following would be the
BEST method of reproducing 800 copies?
    A. An outside private printer, because you can best
       maintain confidentiality using this technique
    B. Xeroxing, because the copies will have the best
       possible appearance
    C. Typing carbon copies, because you will be certain
       that there are the fewest possible errors
    D. The multilith process, because it is quick and neat

22. The files in your office have been overcrowded and diffi-   22. ...
cult to work with since you started working there. One
day your supervisor is transferred and another assistant
in your office decides to discard three drawers of the
oldest materials.
For him to take this action is
    A. *desirable;* it will facilitate handling the more active
       materials
    B. *desirable;* no file should be removed from its point of
       origin

7

    C. *desirable;* there is no need to burden a new super-
       visor with unnecessary information
    D. *undesirable;* no file should be discarded without
       first noting what material has been discarded

23. You have been criticized by the general supervisor because 23. ...
of spelling errors in some of your typing. You have only
copied the reports as written and you realize that the
errors occurred in work given to you by your immediate
supervisor.
Of the following, the BEST way for you to handle this
situation is to
    A. tell the general supervisor that the spelling errors
      are your immediate supervisor's, not yours, because
      they occur only when you type his reports
    B. tell the general supervisor that you only type the
      reports as given to you, without indicating anyone
    C. inform your immediate supervisor that you have been
      unjustly criticized because of his spelling errors
      and politely request that he be more careful in the
      future
    D. use a dictionary whenever you have doubt regarding
      spelling

24. You have recently found several items misfiled. You be- 24. ...
lieve that this occurred because a new assistant in your
section has been making mistakes.
The BEST course of action for you to take is to
    A. refile the material and say nothing about it
    B. send your supervisor an anonymous note of complaint
      about the filing errors
    C. show the errors to the new assistant and tell him
      why they are errors in filing
    D. tell your supervisor that the new assistant makes a
      lot of errors in filing

KEY (CORRECT ANSWERS)

	TEST 1					TEST 2		
1. C		11. C		1. A			11. A
2. D		12. C		2. A			12. B
3. C		13. D		3. B			13. C
4. B		14. D		4. B			14. B
5. B		15. B		5. B			15. C
6. C		16. A		6. B			16. D
7. D		17. A		7. C			17. D
8. A		18. B		8. C			18. B
9. B		19. B		9. B			19. C
10. D		20. A		10. D			20. A
	21. C				21. D		
	22. A				22. D		
	23. C				23. D		
	24. A				24. C		
	25. A						

PREPARING WRITTEN MATERIAL

PARAGRAPH REARRANGEMENT

COMMENTARY

The sentences which follow are in scrambled order. You are to rearrange them in proper order and indicate the letter choice containing the correct answer at the space at the right.

Each group of sentences in this section is actually a paragraph presented in scrambled order. Each sentence in the group has a place in that paragraph; no sentence is to be left out. You are to read each group of sentences and decide upon the best order in which to put the sentences so as to form as well-organized paragraph.

The questions in this section measure the ability to solve a problem when all the facts relevant to its solution are not given.

More specifically, certain positions of responsibility and authority require the employee to discover connections between events sometimes, apparently, unrelated. In order to do this, the employee will find it necessary to correctly infer that unspecified events have probably occurred or are likely to occur. This ability becomes especially important when action must be taken on incomplete information.

Accordingly, these questions require competitors to choose among several suggested alternatives, each of which presents a different sequential arrangement of the events. Competitors must choose the MOST logical of the suggested sequences.

In order to do so, they may be required to draw on general knowledge to infer missing concepts or events that are essential to sequencing the given events. Competitors should be careful to infer only what is essential to the sequence. The plausibility of the wrong alternatives will always require the inclusion of unlikely events or of additional chains of events which are NOT essential to sequencing the given events.

It's very important to remember that you are looking for the best of the four possible choices, and that the best choice of all may not even be one of the answers you're given to choose from.

There is no one right way to these problems. Many people have found it helpful to first write out the order of the sentences, as they would have arranged them, on their scrap paper before looking at the possible answers. If their optimum answer is there, this can save them some time. If it isn't, this method can still give insight into solving the problem. Others find it most helpful to just go through each of the possible choices, contrasting each as they go along. You should use whatever method feels comfortable, and works, for you.

While most of these types of questions are not that difficult, we've added a higher percentage of the difficult type, just to give you more practice. Usually there are only one or two questions on this section that contain such subtle distinctions that you're unable to answer confidently, and you then may find yourself stuck deciding between two possible choices, neither of which you're sure about.

EXAMINATION SECTION
TEST 1

DIRECTIONS: The following groups of sentences need to be arranged in an order that makes sense. Select the letter preceding the sequence that represents the BEST sentence order. *PRINT THE LETTER OF THE CORRECT ANSWER IN THE SPACE AT THE RIGHT.*

1.
    I. The keyboard was purposely designed to be a little awkward to slow typists down.
   II. The arrangement of letters on the keyboard of a typewriter was not designed for the convenience of the typist.
 III. Fortunately, no one is suggesting that a new keyboard be designed right away.
  IV. If one were, we would have to learn to type all over again.
   V. The reason was that the early machines were slower than the typists and would jam easily.

    A. I, III, IV, II, V   B. II, V, I, IV, III
    C. V, I, II, III, IV   D. II, I, V, III, IV

1.___

2.
    I. The majority of the new service jobs are part-time or low-paying.
   II. According to the U.S. Bureau of Labor Statistics, jobs in the service sector constitute 72% of all jobs in this country.
 III. If more and more workers receive less and less money, who will buy the goods and services needed to keep the economy going?
  IV. The service sector is by far the fastest growing part of the United States economy.
   V. Some economists look upon this trend with great concern.

    A. II, IV, I, V, III   B. II, III, IV, I, V
    C. V, IV, II, III, I   D. III, I, II, IV, V

2.___

3.
    I. They can also affect one's endurance.
   II. This can stabilize blood sugar levels, and ensure that the brain is receiving a steady, constant supply of glucose, so that one is *hitting on all cylinders* while taking the test.
 III. By food, we mean real food, not junk food or unhealthy snacks.
  IV. For this reason, it is important not to skip a meal, and to bring food with you to the exam.
   V. One's blood sugar levels can affect how clearly one is able to think and concentrate during an exam.

    A. V, IV, II, III, I   B. V, II, I, IV, III
    C. V, I, IV, III, II   D. V, IV, I, III, II

3.___

4. I. Those who are the embodiment of desire are absorbed in material quests, and those who are the embodiment of feeling are warriors who value power more than possession.
    II. These qualities are in everyone, but in different degrees.
    III. But those who value understanding yearn not for goods or victory, but for knowledge.
    IV. According to Plato, human behavior flows from three main sources: desire, emotion, and knowledge.
    V. In the perfect state, the industrial forces would produce but not rule, the military would protect but not rule, and the forces of knowledge, the philosopher kings, would reign.

4.___

    A. IV, V, I, II, III   B. V, I, II, III, IV
    C. IV, III, II, I, V   D. IV, II, I, III, V

5. I. Of the more than 26,000 tons of garbage produced daily in New York City, 12,000 tons arrive daily at Fresh Kills.
    II. In a month, enough garbage accumulates there to fill the Empire State Building.
    III. In 1937, the Supreme Court halted the practice of dumping the trash of New York City into the sea.
    IV. Although the garbage is compacted, in a few years the mounds of garbage at Fresh Kills will be the highest points south of Maine's Mount Desert Island on the Eastern Seaboard.
    V. Instead, tugboats now pull barges of much of the trash to Staten Island and the largest landfill in the world, Fresh Kills.

5.___

    A. III, V, IV, I, II   B. III, V, II, IV, I
    C. III, V, I, II, IV   D. III, II, V, IV, I

6. I. Communists rank equality very high, but freedom very low.
    II. Unlike communists, conservatives place a high value on freedom and a very low value on equality.
    III. A recent study demonstrated that one way to classify people's political beliefs is to look at the importance placed on two words: freedom and equality.
    IV. Thus, by demonstrating how members of these groups feel about the two words, the study has proved to be useful for political analysts in several European countries.
    V. According to the study, socialists and liberals rank both freedom and equality very high, while fascists rate both very low.

6.___

    A. III, V, I, II, IV   B. III, IV, V, I, II
    C. III, V, IV, II, I   D. III, I, II, IV, V

7.   I. "Can there be anything more amazing than this?"   7.___
    II. If the riddle is successfully answered, his dead
        brothers will be brought back to life.
   III. "Even though man sees those around him dying every
        day," says Dharmaraj, "he still believes and acts as
        if he were immortal."
    IV. "What is the cause of ceaseless wonder?" asks the
        Lord of the Lake.
     V. In the ancient epic, The Mahabharata, a riddle is
        asked of one of the Pandava brothers.

    A. V, II, I, IV, III   B. V, IV, III, I, II
    C. V, II, IV, III, I   D. V, II, IV, I, III

8.   I. On the contrary, the two main theories -- the   8.___
        cooperative (neoclassical) theory and the radical
        (labor theory) -- clearly rest on very different
        assumptions, which have very different ethical
        overtones.
    II. The distribution of income is the primary factor in
        determining the relative levels of material well-
        being that different groups or individuals attain.
   III. Of all issues in economics, the distribution of
        income is one of the most controversial.
    IV. The neoclassical theory tends to support the existing
        income distribution (or minor changes), while the
        labor theory tends to support substantial changes in
        the way income is distributed.
     V. The intensity of the controversy reflects the fact
        that different economic theories are not purely
        neutral, *detached* theories with no ethical or moral
        implications.

    A. II, I, V, IV, III   B. III, II, V, I, IV
    C. III, V, II, I, IV   D. III, V, IV, I, II

9.   I. The pool acts as a broker and ensures that the   9.___
        cheapest power gets used first.
    II. Every six seconds, the pool's computer monitors all
        of the generating stations in the state and decides
        which to ask for more power and which to cut back.
   III. The buying and selling of electrical power is handled
        by the New York Power Pool in Guilderland, New York.
    IV. This is to the advantage of both the buying and
        selling utilities.
     V. The pool began operation in 1970, and consists of
        the state's eight electric utilities.

    A. V, I, II, III, IV   B. IV, II, I, III, V
    C. III, V, I, IV, II   D. V, III, IV, II, I

10.   I. Modern English is much simpler grammatically than   10.___
      Old English.
   II. Finnish grammar is very complicated; there are some
      fifteen cases, for example.
  III. Chinese, a very old language, may seem to be the
      exception, but it is the great number of characters/
      words that must be mastered that makes it so
      difficult to learn, not its grammar.
   IV. The newest literary language -- that is, written as
      well as spoken -- is Finnish, whose literary roots
      go back only to about the middle of the nineteenth
      century.
    V. Contrary to popular belief, the longer a language is
      been in use the simpler its grammar -- not the
      reverse.

A. IV, I, II, III, V   B. V, I, IV, II, III
C. I, II, IV, III, V   D. IV, II, III, I, V

———

KEY (CORRECT ANSWERS)

1. D   6. A
2. A   7. C
3. C   8. B
4. D   9. C
5. C   10. B

———

TEST 2

DIRECTIONS: This type of question tests your ability to recognize
accurate paraphrasing, well-constructed paragraphs,
and appropriate style and tone. It is important that
the answer you select contains only the facts or
concepts given in the original sentences. It is also
important that you be aware of incomplete sentences,
inappropriate transitions, unsupported opinions,
incorrect usage, and illogical sentence order. Paragraphs that do not include all the necessary facts and
concepts, that distort them, or that add new ones are
not considered correct.

The format for this section may vary. Sometimes, long
paragraphs are given, and emphasis is placed on style
and organization. Our first five questions are of this
type. Other times, the paragraphs are shorter, and
there is less emphasis on style and more emphasis on
accurate representation of information. Our second
group of five questions are of this nature.

For each of Questions 1 through 10, select the paragraph
that BEST expresses the ideas contained in the sentences
above it. *PRINT THE LETTER OF THE CORRECT ANSWER IN THE
SPACE AT THE RIGHT.*

1.   I. Listening skills are very important for managers.   1.___
     II. Listening skills are not usually emphasized.
    III. Whenever managers are depicted in books, manuals or
         the media, they are always talking, never listening.
     IV. We'd like you to read the enclosed handout on
         listening skills and to try to consciously apply them
         this week.
      V. We guarantee they will improve the quality of your
         interactions.

      A. Unfortunately, listening skills are not usually
         emphasized for managers. Managers are always depicted
         as talking, never listening. We'd like you to read
         the enclosed handout on listening skills. Please
         try to apply these principles this week. If you do,
         we guarantee they will improve the quality of your
         interactions.
      B. The enclosed handout on listening skills will be
         important improving the quality of your interactions.
         We guarantee it. All you have to do is take some
         time this week to read it and to consciously try to
         apply the principles. Listening skills are very
         important for managers, but they are not usually
         emphasized. Whenever managers are depicted in books,
         manuals or the media, they are always talking, never
         listening.

C. Listening well is one of the most important skills a manager can have, yet it's not usually given much attention. Think about any representation of managers in books, manuals, or in the media that you may have seen. They're always talking, never listening. We'd like you to read the enclosed handout on listening skills and consciously try to apply them the rest of the week. We guarantee you will see a difference in the quality of your interactions.

D. Effective listening, one very important tool in the effective manager's arsenal, is usually not emphasized enough. The usual depiction of managers in books, manuals or the media is one in which they are always talking, never listening. We'd like you to read the enclosed handout and consciously try to apply the information contained therein throughout the rest of the week. We feel sure that you will see a marked difference in the quality of your interactions.

2.

    I. Chekhov wrote three dramatic masterpieces which share   2.___
certain themes and formats: <u>Uncle Vanya</u>, <u>The Cherry Orchard</u>, and <u>The Three Sisters</u>.

  II. They are primarily concerned with the passage of time and how this erodes human aspirations.

III. The plays are haunted by the ghosts of the wasted life.

 IV. The characters are concerned with life's lesser problems; however, such as the inability to make decisions, loyalty to the wrong cause, and the inability to be clear.

  V. This results in a sweet, almost aching, type of a sadness referred to as Chekhovian.

A. Chekhov wrote three dramatic masterpieces: <u>Uncle Vanya</u>, <u>The Cherry Orchard</u>, and <u>The Three Sisters</u>. These masterpieces share certain themes and formats: the passage of time, how time erodes human aspirations, and the ghosts of wasted life. Each masterpiece is characterized by a sweet, almost aching, type of sadness that has become known as Chekhovian. The sweetness of this sadness hinges on the fact that it is not the great tragedies of life which are destroying these characters, but their minor flaws: indecisiveness, misplaced loyalty, unclarity.

B. <u>The Cherry Orchard</u>, <u>Uncle Vanya</u>, and <u>The Three Sisters</u> are three dramatic masterpieces written by Chekhov that use similar formats to explore a common theme. Each is primarily concerned with the way that passing time wears down human aspirations, and each is haunted by the ghosts of the wasted life. The characters are shown struggling futilely with the lesser problems of life: indecisiveness, loyalty to the wrong cause, and the inability to be clear. These struggles create a mood of sweet, almost aching, sadness that has become known as Chekhovian.

C. Chekhov's dramatic masterpieces are, along with The Cherry Orchard, Uncle Vanya, and The Three Sisters. These plays share certain thematic and formal similarities. They are concerned most of all with the passage of time and the way in which time erodes human aspirations. Each play is haunted by the specter of the wasted life. Chekhov's characters are caught, however, by life's lesser snares: indecisiveness, loyalty to the wrong cause, and unclarity. The characteristic mood is a sweet, almost aching type of sadness that has come to be known as Chekhovian.

D. A Chekhovian mood is characterized by sweet, almost aching, sadness. The term comes from three dramatic tragedies by Chekhov which revolve around the sadness of a wasted life. The three masterpieces (Uncle Vanya, The Three Sisters, and The Cherry Orchard) share the same theme and format. The plays are concerned with how the passage of time erodes human aspirations. They are peopled with characters who are struggling with life's lesser problems. These are people who are indecisive, loyal to the wrong causes, or are unable to make themselves clear.

3.   I. Movie previews have often helped producers decide   3.___
           what parts of movies they should take out or leave in.
       II. The first 1933 preview of King Kong was very helpful
           to the producers because many people ran screaming
           from the theater and would not return when four men
           first attacked by Kong were eaten by giant spiders.
      III. The 1950 premiere of Sunset Boulevard resulted in the
           filming of an entirely new beginning, and a delay of
           six months in the film's release.
       IV. In the original opening scene, William Holden was in
           a morgue talking with thirty-six other "corpses" about
           the ways some of them had died.
        V. When he began to tell them of his life with Gloria
           Swanson, the audience found this hilarious, instead
           of taking the scene seriously.

       A. Movie previews have often helped producers decide what
          parts of movies they should leave in or take out. For
          example, the first preview of King Kong in 1933 was
          very helpful. In one scene, four men were first
          attacked by Kong and then eaten by giant spiders.
          Many members of the audience ran screaming from the
          theater and would not return. The premiere of the
          1950 film Sunset Boulevard was also very helpful. In
          the original opening scene, William Holden was in a
          morgue with thirty-six other "corpses," discussing
          the ways some of them had died. When he began to
          tell them of his life with Gloria Swanson, the
          audience found this hilarious. They were supposed to
          take the scene seriously. The result was a delay of
          six months in the release of the film while a new
          beginning was added.

B. Movie previews have often helped producers decide whether they should change various parts of a movie. After the 1933 preview of <u>King Kong</u>, a scene in which four men who had been attacked by Kong were eaten by giant spiders was taken out as many people ran screaming from the theater and would not return. The 1950 premiere of <u>Sunset Boulevard</u> also led to some changes. In the original opening scene, William Holden was in a morgue talking with thirty-six other "corpses" about the ways some of them had died. When he began to tell them of his life with Gloria Swanson, the audience found this hilarious, instead of taking the scene seriously.

C. What do <u>Sunset Boulevard</u> and <u>King Kong</u> have in common? Both show the value of using movie previews to test audience reaction. The first 1933 preview of <u>King Kong</u> showed that a scene showing four men being eaten by giant spiders after having been attacked by Kong was too frightening for many people. They ran screaming from the theater and couldn't be coaxed back. The 1950 premiere of <u>Sunset Boulevard</u> was also a scream, but not the kind the producers intended. The movie opens with William Holden lying in a morgue discussing the ways they had died with thirty-six other "corpses." When he began to tell them of his life with Gloria Swanson, the audience couldn't take him seriously. Their laughter caused a six-month delay while the beginning was rewritten.

D. Producers very often use movie previews to decide if changes are needed. The premiere of <u>Sunset Boulevard</u> in 1950 led to a new beginning and a six-month delay in film release. At the beginning, William Holden and thirty-six other "corpses" discuss the ways some of them died. Rather than taking this seriously, the audience thought it was hilarious when he began to tell them of his life with Gloria Swanson. The first 1933 preview of <u>King Kong</u> was very helpful for its producers because one scene so terrified the audience that many of them ran screaming from the theater and would not return. In this particular scene, four men who had first been attacked by Kong were being eaten by giant spiders.

4.   I. It is common for supervisors to view employees as   4.___
           "things" to be manipulated.
       II. This approach does not motivate employees, nor does
           the carrot-and-stick approach because employees often
           recognize these behaviors and resent them.
      III. Supervisors can change these behaviors by using self-
           inquiry and persistence.
       IV. The best managers genuinely respect those they work
           with, are supportive and helpful, and are interested
           in working as a team with those they supervise.
        V. They disagree with the Golden Rule that says "he or
           she who has the gold makes the rules."

A. Some managers act as if they think the Golden Rule means "he or she who has the gold makes the rules." They show disrespect to employees by seeing them as "things" to be manipulated. Obviously, this approach does not motivate employees any more than the carrot-and-stick approach motivates them. The employees are smart enough to spot these behaviors and resent them. On the other hand, the managers genuinely respect those they work with, are supportive and helpful, and are interested in working as a team. Self-inquiry and persistence can change even the former type of supervisor into the latter.

B. Many supervisors fall into the trap of viewing employees as "things" to be manipulated, or try to motivate them by using a carrot-and-stick approach. These methods do not motivate employees, who often recognize the behaviors and resent them. Supervisors can change these behaviors, however, by using self-inquiry and persistence. The best managers are supportive and helpful, and have genuine respect for those with whom they work. They are interested in working as a team with those they supervise. To them, the Golden Rule is not "he or she who has the gold makes the rules."

C. Some supervisors see employees as "things" to be used or manipulated using a carrot-and-stick technique. These methods don't work. Employees often see through them and resent them. A supervisor who wants to change may do so. The techniques of self-inquiry and persistence can be used to turn him or her into the type of supervisor who doesn't think the Golden Rule is "he or she who has the gold makes the rules." They may become like the best managers who treat those with whom they work with respect and give them help and support. These are the managers who know how to build a team.

D. Unfortunately, many supervisors act as if their employees are objects whose movements they can position at will. This mistaken belief has the same result as another popular motivational technique -- the carrot-and-stick approach. Both attitudes can lead to the same result -- resentment from those employees who recognize the behaviors for what they are. Supervisors who recognize these behaviors can change through the use of persistence and the use of self-inquiry. It's important to remember that the best managers respect their employees. They readily give necessary help and support and are interested in working as a team with those they supervise. To these managers, the Golden Rule is not "he or she who has the gold makes the rules."

5.   I. The first half of the nineteenth century produced a group of pessimistic poets -- Byron, De Musset, Heine, Pushkin, and Leopardi.

  II. It also produced a group of pessimistic composers -- Schubert, Chopin, Schumann, and even the later Beethoven.

III. Above all, in philosophy, there was the profoundly pessimistic philosopher, Schopenhauer.

 IV. The Revolution was dead, the Bourbons were restored, the feudal barons were reclaiming their land, and progress everywhere was being suppressed, as the great age was over.

  V. "I thank God," said Goethe, "that I am not young in so thoroughly finished a world."

A. "I thank God," said Goethe, "that I am not young in so thoroughly finished a world." The Revolution was dead, the Bourbons were restored, the feudal barons were reclaiming their land, and progress everywhere was being suppressed. The first half of the nineteenth century produced a group of pessimistic poets: Byron, De Musset, Heine, Pushkin, and Leopardi. It also produced pessimistic composers: Schubert, Chopin, Schumann. Although Beethoven came later, he fits into this group, too. Finally and above all, it also produced a profoundly pessimistic philosopher, Schopenhauer. The great age was over.

B. The first half of the nineteenth century produced a group of pessimistic poets: Byron, De Musset, Heine, Pushkin, and Leopardi. It produced a group of pessimistic composers: Schubert, Chopin, Schumann, and even the later Beethoven. Above all, it produced a profoundly pessimistic philosopher, Schopenhauer. For each of these men, the great age was over. The Revolution was dead, and the Bourbons were restored. The feudal barons were reclaiming their land, and progress everywhere was being suppressed.

C. The great age was over. The Revolution was dead -- the Bourbons were restored, and the feudal barons were reclaiming their land. Progress everywhere was being suppressed. Out of this climate came a profound pessimism. Poets, like Byron, De Musset, Heine, Pushkin, and Leopardi; composers, like Schubert, Chopin, Schumann, and even the later Beethoven; and, above all, a profoundly pessimistic philosopher, Schopenauer. This pessimism which arose in the first half of the nineteenth century is illustrated by these words of Goethe, "I thank God that I am not young in so thoroughly finished a world."

D. The first half of the nineteenth century produced a group of pessimistic poets, Byron, De Musset, Heine, Pushkin, and Leopardi -- and a group of pessimistic composers, Schubert, Chopin, Schumann, and the later Beethoven. Above all, it produced a profoundly

pessimistic philosopher, Schopenhauer. The great age
was over. The Revolution was dead, the Bourbons were
restored, the feudal barons were reclaiming their
land, and progress everywhere was being suppressed.
"I thank God," said Goethe, "that I am not young in
so thoroughly finished a world."

6.
  I. A new manager sometimes may feel insecure about his
     or her competence in the new position.
 II. The new manager may then exhibit defensive or arro-
     gant behavior towards those one supervises, or the
     new manager may direct overly flattering behavior
     toward one's new supervisor.

    6.___

  A. Sometimes, a new manager may feel insecure about his
     or her ability to perform well in this new position.
     The insecurity may lead him or her to treat others
     differently. He or she may display arrogant or
     defensive behavior towards those he or she supervises,
     or be overly flattering to his or her new supervisor.
  B. A new manager may sometimes feel insecure about his or
     her ability to perform well in the new position. He
     or she may then become arrogant, defensive, or overly
     flattering towards those he or she works with.
  C. There are times when a new manager may be insecure
     about how well he or she can perform in the new job.
     The new manager may also behave defensive or act in
     an arrogant way towards those he or she supervises, or
     overly flatter his or her boss.
  D. Sometimes, a new manager may feel insecure about his
     or her ability to perform well in the new position.
     He or she may then display arrogant or defensive
     behavior towards those they supervise, or become
     overly flattering towards their supervisors.

7.
  I. It is possible to eliminate unwanted behavior by
     bringing it under stimulus control -- tying the
     behavior to a cue, and then never, or rarely, giving
     the cue.
 II. One trainer successfully used this method to keep an
     energetic young porpoise from coming out of her tank
     whenever she felt like it, which was potentially
     dangerous.
III. Her trainer taught her to do it for a reward, in
     response to a hand signal, and then rarely gave the
     signal.

    7.___

  A. Unwanted behavior can be eliminated by tying the
     behavior to a cue, and then never, or rarely, giving
     the cue. This is called stimulus control. One trainer
     was able to use this method to keep an energetic
     young porpoise from coming out of her tank by teaching
     her to come out for a reward in response to a hand
     signal, and then rarely giving the signal.

B. Stimulus control can be used to eliminate unwanted behavior. In this method, behavior is tied to a cue, and then the cue is rarely, if ever, given. One trainer was able to successfully use stimulus control to keep an energetic young porpoise from coming out of her tank whenever she felt like it -- a potentially dangerous practice. She taught the porpoise to come out for a reward when she gave a hand signal, and then rarely gave the signal.

C. It is possible to eliminate behavior that is undesirable by bringing it under stimulus control by tying behavior to a signal, and then rarely giving the signal. One trainer successfully used this method to keep an energetic young porpoise from coming out of her tank, a potentially dangerous situation. Her trainer taught the porpoise to do it for a reward, in response to a hand signal, and then would rarely give the signal.

D. By using stimulus control, it is possible to eliminate unwanted behavior by tying the behavior to a cue, and then rarely or never give the cue. One trainer was able to use this method to successfully stop a young porpoise from coming out of her tank whenever she felt like it. To curb this potentially dangerous practice, the porpoise was taught by the trainer to come out of the tank for a reward, in response to a hand signal, and then rarely given the signal.

8.   I. There is a great deal of concern over the safety of   8.___
commercial trucks, caused by their greatly increased role in serious accidents since federal deregulation in 1981.

   II. Recently, 60 percent of trucks in New York and Connecticut and 70 percent of trucks in Maryland randomly stopped by state troopers failed safety inspections.

  III. Sixteen states in the United States require no training at all for truck drivers.

   A. Since federal deregulation in 1981, there has been a great deal of concern over the safety of commercial trucks, and their greatly increased role in serious accidents. Recently, 60 percent of trucks in New York and Connecticut, and 70 percent of trucks in Maryland failed safety inspections. Sixteen states in the United States require no training at all for truck drivers.

   B. There is a great deal of concern over the safety of commercial trucks since federal deregulation in 1981. Their role in serious accidents has greatly increased. Recently, 60 percent of trucks randomly stopped in Connecticut and New York, and 70 percent in Maryland failed safety inspections conducted by state troopers. Sixteen states in the United States provide no training at all for truck drivers.

C. Commercial trucks have a greatly increased role in serious accidents since federal deregulation in 1981. This has led to a great deal of concern. Recently, 70 percent of trucks in Maryland and 60 percent of trucks in New York and Connecticut failed inspection of those that were randomly stopped by state troopers. Sixteen states in the United States require no training for all truck drivers.

D. Since federal deregulation in 1981, the role that commercial trucks have played in serious accidents has greatly increased, and this has led to a great deal of concern. Recently, 60 percent of trucks in New York and Connecticut, and 70 percent of trucks in Maryland randomly stopped by state troopers failed safety inspections. Sixteen states in the U.S. don't require any training for truck drivers.

9.
   I. No matter how much some people have, they still feel unsatisfied and want more, or want to keep what they have forever.
  II. One recent television documentary showed several people flying from New York to Paris for a one-day shopping spree to buy platinum earrings, because they were bored.
III. In Brazil, some people are ordering coffins that cost a minimum of $45,000 and are equipping them with deluxe stereos, televisions and other graveyard necessities.

9.___

A. Some people, despite having a great deal, still feel unsatisfied and want more, or think they can keep what they have forever. One recent documentary on television showed several people enroute from Paris to New York for a one day shopping spree to buy platinum earrings, because they were bored. Some people in Brazil are even ordering coffins equipped with such graveyard necessities as deluxe stereos and televisions. The price of the coffins start at $45,000.

B. No matter how much some people have, they may feel unsatisfied. This leads them to want more, or to want to keep what they have forever. Recently, a television documentary depicting several people flying from New York to Paris for a one day shopping spree to buy platinum earrings. They were bored. Some people in Brazil are ordering coffins that cost at least $45,000 and come equipped with deluxe televisions, stereos and other necessary graveyard items.

C. Some people will be dissatisfied no matter how much they have. They may want more, or they may want to keep what they have forever. One recent television documentary showed several people, motivated by boredom, jetting from New York to Paris for a one-day shopping spree to buy platinum earrings. In Brazil, some people are ordering coffins equipped with deluxe stereos, televisions and other graveyard necessities. The minimum price for these coffins - $45,000.

D. Some people are never satisfied. No matter how much they have they still want more, or think they can keep what they have forever. One television documentary recently showed several people flying from New York to Paris for the day to buy platinum earrings because they were bored. In Brazil, some people are ordering coffins that cost $45,000 and are equipped with deluxe stereos, televisions and other graveyard necessities.

10.   I. A television signal or video signal has three parts.   10.___

    II. Its parts are the black-and-white portion, the color portion, and the synchronizing (sync) pulses, which keep the picture stable.

  III. Each video source, whether it's a camera or a video-cassette recorder, contains its own generator of these synchronizing pulses to accompany the picture that it's sending in order to keep it steady and straight.

  IV. In order to produce a clean recording, a video-cassette recorder must "lock-up" to the sync pulses that are part of the video it is trying to record, and this effort may be very noticeable if the device does not have genlock.

A. There are three parts to a television or video signal: the black-and-white part, the color part, and the synchronizing (sync) pulses, which keep the picture stable. Whether it's a video-cassette recorder or a camera, each each video source contains its own pulse that synchronizes and generates the picture it's sending in order to keep it straight and steady. A video-cassette recorder must "lock up" to the sync pulses that are part of the video it's trying to record. If the device doesn't have genlock, this effort must be very noticeable.

B. A video signal or television is comprised of three parts: the black-and-white portion, the color por-tion, and the the sync (synchronizing) pulses, which keep the picture stable. Whether it's a camera or a video-cassette recorder, each video source contains its own generator of these synchronizing pulses. These accompany the picture that it's sending in order to keep it straight and steady. A video-cassette recorder must "lock up" to the sync pulses that are part of the video it is trying to record in order to produce a clean recording. This effort may be very noticeable if the device does not have genlock.

C. There are three parts to a television or video signal: the color portion, the black-and-white portion, and the sync (synchronizing pulses). These keep the picture stable. Each video source, whether it's a video-cassette recorder or a camera, generates these synchronizing pulses accompanying the picture it's sending in order to keep it straight and steady. If a clean recording is to be produced, a video-cassette recorder must store the sync pulses that are part of the video it is trying to record. This effort may not be noticeable if the device does not have gen-lock.

D. A television signal or video signal has three parts: the black-and-white portion, the color portion, and the synchronizing (sync) pulses. It's the sync pulses which keep the picture stable, which accompany it and keep it steady and straight. Whether it's a camera or a video-cassette recorder, each video source contains its own generator of these synchronizing pulses. To produce a clean recording, a video-cassette recorder must "lock-up" to the sync pulses that are part of the video it is trying to record. If the device does not have genlock, this effort may be very noticeable.

—————

KEY (CORRECT ANSWERS)

1.	C	6.	A
2.	B	7.	B
3.	A	8.	D
4.	B	9.	C
5.	D	10.	D

—————

INTERPRETING STATISTICAL DATA
GRAPHS, CHARTS AND TABLES

DIRECTIONS: Each question or incomplete statement is followed by several suggested answers or completions. Select the one that BEST answers the question or completes the statement. *PRINT THE LETTER OF THE CORRECT ANSWER IN THE SPACE AT THE RIGHT.*

TEST 1

Questions 1-3.

DIRECTIONS: Questions 1 through 3 are to be answered SOLELY on the basis of the following table.

QUARTERLY SALES REPORTED BY MAJOR INDUSTRY GROUPS
DECEMBER 1997 - FEBRUARY 1999

Industry Groups	Reported Sales, Taxable & Non-Taxable (In Millions)				
	12/97-2/98	3/98-5/98	6/98-8/98	9/98-11/98	12/98-2/99
Retailers	2,802	2,711	2,475	2,793	2,974
Wholesalers	2,404	2,237	2,269	2,485	2,512
Manufacturers	3,016	2,888	3,001	3,518	3,293
Services	1,034	1,065	984	1,132	1,092

1. The trend in total reported sales may be described as   1.___
    A. downward   B. downward and upward
    C. horizontal   D. upward

2. The two industry groups that reveal a similar seasonal   2.___
    pattern for the period December 1997 through November 1998
    are
    A. retailers and manufacturers
    B. retailers and wholesalers
    C. wholesalers and manufacturers
    D. wholesalers and service

3. Reported sales were at a MINIMUM between   3.___
    A. December 1997 and February 1998
    B. March 1998 and May 1998
    C. June 1998 and August 1998
    D. September 1998 and November 1998

TEST 2

DIRECTIONS: Questions 1 through 4 are to be answered SOLELY on the basis of the following information.

The income elasticity of demand for selected items of consumer demand in the United States are:

Item	Elasticity
Airline Travel	5.66
Alcohol	.62
Dentist Fees	1.00
Electric Utilities	3.00
Gasoline	1.29
Intercity Bus	1.89
Local Bus	1.41
Restaurant Meals	.75

1. The demand for the item listed below that would be MOST adversely affected by a decrease in income is
   A. alcohol   B. electric utilities
   C. gasoline   D. restaurant meals

   1.___

2. The item whose relative change in demand would be the same as the relative change in income would be
   A. dentist fees   B. gasoline
   C. restaurant meals   D. none of the above

   2.___

3. If income increases by 12 percent, the demand for restaurant meals may be expected to increase by
   A. 9 percent   B. 12 percent
   C. 16 percent   D. none of the above

   3.___

4. On the basis of the above information, the item whose demand would be MOST adversely affected by an increase in the sales tax from 7 percent to 8 percent to be passed on to the consumer in the form of higher prices
   A. would be airline travel   B. would be alcohol
   C. would be gasoline   D. cannot be determined

   4.___

TEST 3

Questions 1-3.

DIRECTIONS: Questions 1 through 3 are to be answered SOLELY on the basis of the following graphs depicting various relationships in a single retail store.

GRAPH I
RELATIONSHIP BETWEEN NUMBER OF CUSTOMERS IN STORE AND TIME OF DAY

GRAPH II
RELATIONSHIP BETWEEN NUMBER OF CHECK-OUT LANES AVAILABLE IN STORE AND WAIT TIME FOR CHECK-OUT

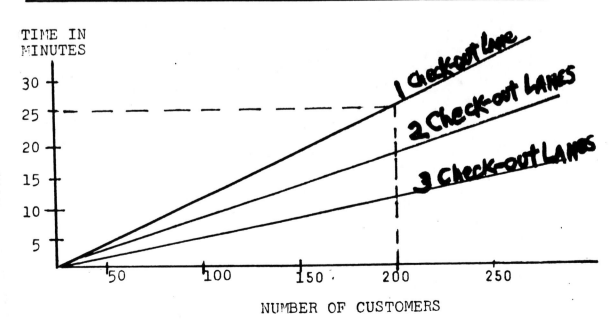

Note the dotted lines in Graph II. They demonstrate that, if there are 200 people in the store and only 1 check-out lane is open, the wait time will be 25 minutes.

3

1. At what time would a person be most likely NOT to have to   1.___
   wait more than 15 minutes if only one check-out lane is
   open?
      A. 11 A.M.   B. 12 Noon   C. 1 P.M.   D. 3 P.M.

2. At what time of day would a person have to wait the   2.___
   LONGEST to check out if 3 check-out lanes are available?
      A. 11 A.M.   B. 12 Noon   C. 1 P.M.   D. 2 P.M.

3. The difference in wait times between 1 and 3 check-out   3.___
   lanes at 3 P.M. is MOST NEARLY
      A. 5   B. 10   C. 15   D. 20

———

4

TEST 4

Questions 1-4.

DIRECTIONS: Questions 1 through 4 are to be answered SOLELY on
the basis of the graph below.

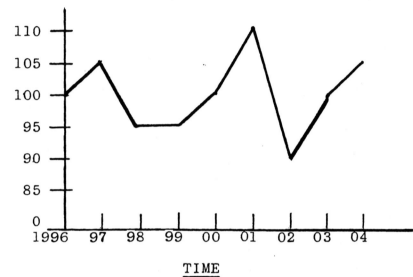

Number of
data
sheets
per hour

(based on
20 entries
per sheet)

TIME

1. Of the following, during what four-year period did the   1.___
   average output of computer operators fall BELOW 100 sheets
   per hour?
       A. 1997-00   B. 1998-01   C. 2000-03   D. 2001-04

2. The average percentage change in output over the previous   2.___
   year's output for the years 1999 to 2002 is MOST NEARLY
       A. 2   B. 0   C. -5   C. -7

3. The difference between the actual output for 2002 and the   3.___
   projected figure based upon the average increase from
   1996-2001 is MOST NEARLY
       A. 18   B. 20   C. 22   D. 24

4. Assume that after constructing the above graph you, an   4.___
   analyst, discovered that the average number of entries
   per sheet in 2002 was 25 (instead of 20) because
   of the complex nature of the work performed during that
   period.
   The average output in cards per hour for the period 2000-
   03, expressed in terms of 20 items per sheet, would then
   be MOST NEARLY
       A. 95   B. 100   C. 105   D. 110

5

TEST 5

DIRECTIONS: Questions 1 through 3 are to be answered on the basis
of the following data assembled for a cost-benefit
analysis.

	Cost	Benefit
No program	0	0
Alternative W	$ 3,000	$ 6,000
Alternative X	$10,000	$17,000
Alternative Y	$17,000	$25,000
Alternative Z	$30,000	$32,000

1. From the point of view of selecting the alternative with   1.___
    the best cost benefit ratio, the BEST alternative is
    Alternative
    A. W   B. X   C. Y   D. Z

2. From the point of view of selecting the alternative with   2.___
    the best measure of net benefit, the BEST alternative is
    Alternative
    A. W   B. X   C. Y   D. Z

3. From the point of view of pushing public expenditure to   3.___
    the point where marginal benefit equals or exceeds
    marginal cost, the BEST alternative is Alternative
    A. W   B. X   C. Y   D. Z

TEST 6

Questions 1-3.

DIRECTIONS: Questions 1 through 3 are to be answered SOLELY on
the basis of the following data.

A series of cost-benefit studies of various alternative health
programs yields the following results:

Program	Benefit	Cost
K	30	15
L	60	60
M	300	150
N	600	500

In answering Questions 1 and 2, assume that all programs can
be increased or decreased in scale without affecting their individual
benefit-to-cost ratios.

1. The benefit-to-cost ratio of Program M is   1.___
   A. 10:1   B. 5:1   C. 2:1   D. 1:2

2. The budget ceiling for one or more of the programs   2.___
   included in the study is set at 75 units.
   It may MOST logically be concluded that
   A. Programs K and L should be chosen to fit within the
      budget ceiling
   B. Program K would be the most desirable one that could
      be afforded
   C. Program M should be chosen rather than Program K
   D. the choice should be between Programs M and K

3. If no assumptions can be made regarding the effects of   3.___
   change of scale, the MOST logical conclusion, on the
   basis of the data available, is that
   A. more data are needed for a budget choice of program
   B. Program K is the most preferable because of its low
      cost and good benefit-to-cost ratio
   C. Program M is the most preferable because of its
      high benefits and good benefit-to-cost ratio
   D. there is no difference between Programs K and M, and
      either can be chosen for any purpose

TEST 7

Questions 1-6.

DIRECTIONS: Questions 1 through 6 are to be answered SOLELY on the basis of the information contained in the charts below which relate to the budget allocations of City X, a small suburban community. The charts depict the annual budget allocations by Department and by expenditures over a five-year period.

CITY X BUDGET IN MILLIONS OF DOLLARS

TABLE I.   Budget Allocations By Department

Department	1997	1998	1999	2000	2001
Public Safety	30	45	50	40	50
Health and Welfare	50	75	90	60	70
Engineering	5	8	10	5	8
Human Resources	10	12	20	10	22
Conservation & Environment	10	15	20	20	15
Education & Development	15	25	35	15	15
TOTAL BUDGET	120	180	225	150	180

TABLE II.   Budget Allocations by Expenditures

Category	1997	1998	1999	2000	2001
Raw Materials & Machinery	36	63	68	30	98
Capital Outlay	12	27	56	15	18
Personal Services	72	90	101	105	64
TOTAL BUDGET	120	180	225	150	180

1. The year in which the SMALLEST percentage of the total annual budget was allocated to the Department of Education and Development is
   A. 1997   B. 1998   C. 2000   D. 2001

2. Assume that in 2000 the Department of Conservation and Environment divided its annual budget into the three categories of expenditures and in exactly the same proportion as the budget shown in Table II for the year 2000. The amount allocated for capital outlay in the Department of Conservation and Environment's 2000 budget was MOST NEARLY _____ million.
   A. $2   B. $4   C. $6   D. $10

8

3. From the year 1998 to the year 2000, the sum of the   3.____
   annual budgets for the Departments of Public Safety and
   Engineering showed an overall _____ of _____ million.
      A. decline; $8   B. increase; $7
      C. decline; $15   D. increase; $22

4. The LARGEST dollar increase in departmental budget alloca-   4.____
   tions from one year to the next was in _____ from _____.
      A. Public Safety; 1997 to 1998
      B. Health and Welfare; 1997 to 1998
      C. Education and Development; 1999 to 2000
      D. Human Resources; 1999 to 2000

5. During the five-year period, the annual budget of the   5.____
   Department of Human Resources was GREATER than the annual
   budget for the Department of Conservation and Environment
   in _____ of the years.
      A. none   B. one   C. two   D. three

6. If the total City X budget increases at the same rate from   6.____
   2001 to 2002 as it did from 2000 to 2001, the total City X
   budget for 2002 will be MOST NEARLY _____ million.
      A. $180   B. $200   C. $210   D. $215

———

TEST 8

Questions 1-3.

DIRECTIONS: Questions 1 through 3 are to be answered SOLELY on the basis of the following information.

Assume that in order to encourage Program A, the State and Federal governments have agreed to make the following reimbursements for money spent on Program A, provided the unreimbursed balance is paid from City funds.

During Fiscal Year 2001-2002 - For the first $2 million expended, 50% Federal reimbursement and 30% State reimbursement; for the next $3 million, 40% Federal reimbursement and 20% State reimbursement; for the next $5 million, 20% Federal reimbursement and 10% State reimbursement. Above $10 million expended, no Federal or State reimbursement.

During Fiscal Year 2002-2003 - For the first $1 million expended, 30% Federal reimbursement and 20% State reimbursement; for the next $4 million, 15% Federal reimbursement and 10% State reimbursement. Above $5 million expended, no Federal or State reimbursement.

1. Assume that the Program A expenditures are such that the   1.___
    State reimbursement for Fiscal Year 2001-2002 will be
    $1 million.
    Then, the Federal reimbursement for Fiscal Year 2001-2002
    will be
        A. $1,600,000   B. $1,800,000
        C. $2,000,000   D. $2,600,000

2. Assume that $8 million were to be spent on Program A in   2.___
    Fiscal Year 2002-2003.
    The TOTAL amount of unreimbursed City funds required would
    be
        A. $3,500,000   B. $4,500,000
        C. $5,500,000   D. $6,500,000

3. Assume that the City desires to have a combined total of   3.___
    $6 million spent in Program A during both the Fiscal Year
    2001-2002 and the Fiscal Year 2002-2003.
    Of the following expenditure combinations, the one which
    results in the GREATEST reimbursement of City funds is
    _____ in Fiscal Year 2001-2002 and _____ in Fiscal Year
    2002-2003.
        A. $5 million; $1 million   B. $4 million; $2 million
        C. $3 million; $3 million   D. $2 million; $4 million

KEY (CORRECT ANSWERS)

TEST 1

1. D
2. C
3. C

TEST 2

1. B
2. A
3. A
4. D

TEST 3

1. A
2. D
3. B

TEST 4

1. A
2. B
3. C
4. C

TEST 5

1. A
2. C
3. C

TEST 6

1. C
2. D
3. A

TEST 7

1. D
2. A
3. A
4. B
5. B
6. D

TEST 8

1. B
2. D
3. A

PRINCIPLES AND PRACTICES OF ADMINISTRATION, SUPERVISION & MANAGEMENT

CONTENTS

CONTENTS (CONT.)

PRINCIPLES AND PRACTICES OF

ADMINISTRATION, SUPERVISION & MANAGEMENT

Most people are inclined to think of administration as something that only a few persons are responsible for in a large organization. Perhaps this is true if you are thinking of Administration with a capital *A*, but administration with a lower case *a* is a responsibility of supervisors at all levels each working day.

All of us feel we are pretty good supervisors and that we do a good job of administering the workings of our agency. By and large, this is true, but every so often it is good to check up on ourselves. Checklists appear from time to time in various publications which psychologists say, tell whether or not a person will make a good wife, husband, doctor, lawyer, or supervisor.

The following questions are an excellent checklist to test yourself as a supervisor and administrator.

Remember, Administration gives direction and points the way but administration carries the ideas to fruition. Each is dependent on the other for its success. Remember, too, that no unit is too small for these departmental functions to be carried out. These statements apply equally as well to the Chief Librarian as to the Department Head with but one or two persons to supervise.

GENERAL ADMINISTRATION - General Responsibilities of Supervisors

1. Have I prepared written statements of functions, activities, and duties for my organizational unit?

2. Have I prepared procedural guides for operating activities?

3. Have I established clearly in writing, lines of authority and responsibility for my organizational unit?

4. Do I make recommendations for improvements in organization, policies, administrative and operating routines and procedures, including simplification of work and elimination of non-essential operations?

5. Have I designated and trained an understudy to function in my absence?

6. Do I supervise and train personnel within the unit to effectively perform their assignments?

7. Do I assign personnel and distribute work on such a basis as to carry out the organizational unit's assignment or mission in the most effective and efficient manner?

8. Have I established administrative controls by:

    a. Fixing responsibility and accountability on all super-
        visors under my direction for the proper performance
        of their functions and duties.

    b. Preparing and submitting periodic work load and progress
        reports covering the operations of the unit to my
        immediate superior.

    c. Analysis and evaluation of such reports received from
        subordinate units.

    d. Submission of significant developments and problems
        arising within the organizational unit to my immediate
        superior.

    e. Conducting conferences, inspections, etc., as to the
        status and efficiency of unit operations.

9. Do I maintain an adequate and competent working force?

10. Have I fostered good employee-department relations, seeing
that established rules, regulations, and instructions are being
carried out properly?

11. Do I collaborate and consult with other organizational units
performing related functions to insure harmonious and efficient
working relationships?

12. Do I maintain liaison through prescribed channels with city
departments and other governmental agencies concerned with the
activities of the unit?

13. Do I maintain contact with and keep abreast of the latest
developments and techniques of administration (professional societies,
groups, periodicals, etc.) as to their applicability to the activities
of the unit?

14. Do I communicate with superiors and subordinates through
prescribed organizational channels?

15. Do I notify superiors and subordinates in instances where
bypassing is necessary as soon thereafter as practicable?

16. Do I keep my superior informed of significant developments
and problems?

SEVEN BASIC FUNCTIONS OF THE SUPERVISOR

1. PLANNING
   This means working out goals and means to obtain goals. What needs to be done, who will do it, how, when, and where it is to be done.

   SEVEN STEPS IN PLANNING

   1. Define job or problem clearly.
   2. Consider priority of job.
   3. Consider time-limit - starting and completing.
   4. Consider minimum distraction to, or interference with, other activities.
   5. Consider and provide for contingencies - possible emergencies.
   6. Break job down into components.
   7. Consider the 5 W's and H:

      WHY   ... is it necessary to do the job? (Is the purpose clearly defined?)
      WHAT ... needs to be done to accomplish the defined purpose?
            ... is needed to do the job? (money, materials, etc.)
      WHO   ... is needed to do the job?
            ... will have responsibilities?
      WHERE ... is the work to be done?
      WHEN ... is the job to begin and end? (schedules, etc.)
      HOW   ... is the job to be done? (methods, controls, records, etc.)

2. ORGANIZING
   This means dividing up the work, establishing clear lines of responsibility and authority and coordinating efforts to get the job done.

3. STAFFING
   The whole personnel function of bringing in and training staff, getting the right man and fitting him to the right job - the job to which he is best suited.
   In the normal situation, the supervisor's responsibility regarding staffing normally includes providing accurate job descriptions, that is, duties of the jobs, requirements, education and experience, skills, physical, etc.; assigning the work for maximum use of skills; and proper utilization of the probationary period to weed out unsatisfactory employees.

4. DIRECTING
   Providing the necessary leadership to the group supervised. Important work gets done to the supervisor's satisfaction.

5. COORDINATING
   The all-important duty of inter-relating the various parts of the work.
   The supervisor is also responsible for controlling the

coordinated activities. This means measuring performance according to a time schedule and setting quotas to see that the goals previously set are being reached. Reports from workers should be analyzed, evaluated, and made part of all future plans.

6. <u>REPORTING</u>
This means proper and effective communication to your superiors, subordinates, and your peers (in definition of the job of the supervisor). Reports should be read and information contained therein should be used ——— not be filed away and forgotten. Reports should be written in such a way that the desired action recommended by the report is forthcoming.

7. <u>BUDGETING</u>
This means controlling current costs and forecasting future costs. This forecast is based on past experience, future plans and programs, as well as current costs.

You will note that these seven functions can fall under three topics:

       Planning   )
       Organizing) Make a plan

       Staffing   )
       Directing   ) Get things done
       Controlling)

       Reporting)
       Budgeting) Watch it work

PLANNING TO MEET MANAGEMENT GOALS

I. <u>WHAT IS PLANNING?</u>
   A. Thinking a job through before new work is done to determine the best way to do it
   B. A method of doing something
   C. Ways and means for achieving set goals
   D. A means of enabling a supervisor to deliver with a minimum of effort, all details involved in coordinating his work

II. <u>WHO SHOULD MAKE PLANS?</u>
Everybody!
All levels of supervision must plan work. (Top management, heads of divisions or bureaus, first line supervisors, and individual employees.) The higher the level, the more planning required.

III. <u>WHAT ARE THE RESULTS OF POOR PLANNING?</u>
   A. Failure to meet deadline
   B. Low employee morale
   C. Lack of job coordination
   D. Overtime is frequently necessary
   E. Excessive cost, waste of material and manhours

IV. PRINCIPLES OF PLANNING
    A. Getting a clear picture of your objectives. What exactly are you trying to accomplish?
    B. Plan the whole job, then the parts, in proper sequence.
    C. Delegate the planning of details to those responsible for executing them.
    D. Make your plan flexible.
    E. Coordinate your plan with the plans of others so that the work may be processed with a minimum of delay.
    F. Sell your plan before you execute it.
    G. Sell your plan to your superior, subordinate, in order to gain maximum participation and coordination.
    H. Your plan should take precedence. Use knowledge and skills that others have brought to a similar job.
    I. Your plan should take account of future contingencies; allow for future expansion.
    J. Plans should include minor details. Leave nothing to chance that can be anticipated.
    K. Your plan should be simple and provide standards and controls. Establish quality and quantity standards and set a standard method of doing the job. The controls will indicate whether the job is proceeding according to plan.
    L. Consider possible bottlenecks, breakdowns, or other difficulties that are likely to arise.

V. Q. WHAT ARE THE *YARDSTICKS* BY WHICH PLANNING SHOULD BE MEASURED?
    A. Any plan should:
    - Clearly state a definite course of action to be followed and goal to be achieved, with consideration for emergencies.
    - Be realistic and practical.
    - State what's to be done, when it's to be done, where, how, and by whom.
    - Establish the most efficient sequence of operating steps so that more is accomplished in less time, with the least effort, and with the best quality results.
    - Assure meeting deliveries without delays.
    - Establish the standard by which performance is to be judged.

    Q. WHAT KINDS OF PLANS DOES EFFECTIVE SUPERVISION REQUIRE?
    A. Plans should cover such factors as:
    - Manpower - right number of properly trained employees on the job.
    - Materials - adequate supply of the right materials and supplies.
    - Machines - full utilization of machines and equipment, with proper maintenance.
    - Methods - most efficient handling of operations.
    - Deliveries - making deliveries on time.
    - Tools - sufficient well-conditioned tools
    - Layout - most effective use of space.
    - Reports - maintaining proper records and reports.
    - Supervision - planning work for employees and organizing supervisor's own time.

MANAGEMENT PRINCIPLES

I. <u>MANAGEMENT</u>

Question: *What do we mean by management?*
Answer: *Getting work done through others.*

Management could also be defined as planning, directing, and controlling the operations of a bureau or division so that all factors will function properly and all persons cooperate efficiently for a common objective.

II. <u>MANAGEMENT PRINCIPLES</u>

1. There should be a hierarchy - wherein authority and responsibility run upward and downward through several levels - with a broad base at the bottom and a single head at the top.

2. Each and every unit or person in the organization should be answerable ultimately to the manager at the apex. In other words, *The buck stops here!*

3. Every necessary function involved in the bureau's objectives is assigned to a unit in that bureau.

4. Responsibilities assigned to a unit are specifically clear-cut and understood.

5. Consistent methods of organizational structure should be applied at each level of the organization.

6. Each member of the bureau from top to bottom knows:
   to whom he reports
   who reports to him.

7. No member of one bureau reports to more than one supervisor.
   No dual functions

8. Responsibility for a function is matched by authority necessary to perform that function.
   Weight of authority

9. Individuals or units reporting to a supervisor do not exceed the number which can be feasibly and effectively coordinated and directed.
   Concept of *span of control*

10. Channels of command (management) are not violated by staff units, although there should be staff services to facilitate and coordinate management functions.

11. Authority and responsibility should be decentralized to units and individuals who are responsible for the actual performance of operations.
    Welfare - down to Welfare Centers
    Hospitals - down to local hospitals

12. Management should exercise control through attention to policy problems of exceptional importance, rather than through review of routine actions of subordinates.

13. Organizations should never be permitted to grow so elaborate as to hinder work accomplishments.
    Empire building

III. <u>ORGANIZATION STRUCTURE</u>
<u>Types of Organizations</u>.
The purest form is a leader and a few followers, such as:

| Supervisor |

| Worker | | Worker | | Worker | | Worker |

(Refer to organization chart) from supervisor to workers.

The line of authority is direct. The workers know exactly where they stand in relation to their boss, to whom they report for instructions and direction.

Unfortunately, in our present complex society, few organizations are similar to this example of a pure line organization. In this era of specialization, other people are often needed in the simplest of organizations. These specialists are known as staff. The sole purpose for their existence (staff) is to assist, advise, suggest, help or counsel line organizations.

Staff has no authority to direct line people - nor do they give them direct instructions.

```
                    ┌──────────┐
                    │SUPERVISOR│
                    └──────────┘
                         │
   ┌─────────────┬───────┴───────┬──────────────┐
┌─────────┐ ┌──────────┐ ┌────────────┐ ┌───────┐
│Personnel│ │Accounting│ │ Inspection │ │ Legal │
└─────────┘ └──────────┘ └────────────┘ └───────┘
 ┌────────┐   ┌────────┐   ┌────────┐   ┌────────┐
 │ Worker │   │ Worker │   │ Worker │   │ Worker │
 └────────┘   └────────┘   └────────┘   └────────┘
```

Line Functions

1. Directs
2. Orders
3. Responsibility for carrying out activities from beginning to end
4. Follows chain of command
5. Is identified with what it does
6. Decides when and how to use staff advice
7. Line executes

Staff Functions

1. Advises
2. Persuades and sells
3. Staff studies, reports, recommends but does not carry out
4. May advise across department lines
5. May find its ideas identified with others
6. Has to persuade line to want its advice
7. Staff - Conducts studies and research. Provides advice and instructions in technical matters. Serves as technical specialist to render specific services

Types and Functions of Organization Charts.
An organization chart is a picture of the arrangement and inter-relationship of the subdivisions of an organization.

1. Types of Charts:
   a. Structural - basic relationships only
   b. Functional - includes functions or duties
   c. Personnel - positions, salaries, status, etc.
   d. Process Chart - work performed
   e. Gantt Chart - actual performance against planned
   f. Flow Chart - flow and distribution of work

2. Functions of Charts:
   a. Assist in management planning and control
   b. Indicate duplication of functions
   c. Indicate incorrect stressing of functions
   d. Indicate neglect of important functions
   e. Correct unclear authority
   f. Establish proper span of control

3. Limitations of Charts:
   a. Seldom maintained on current basis
   b. Chart is oversimplified
   c. Human factors cannot adequately be charted

4. Organization Charts should be:
   a. Simple
   b. Symmetrical
   c. Indicate authority
   d. Line and staff relationship differentiated
   e. Chart should be dated and bear signature of approving officer
   f. Chart should be displayed, not hidden

ORGANIZATION

There are four basic principles of organization:

1. Unity of command
2. Span of control
3. Uniformity of assignment
4. Assignment of responsibility and delegation of authority

Unity of Command

Unity of command means that each person in the organization should receive orders from one, and only one, supervisor. When a person has to take orders from two or more people, (a) the orders may be in conflict and the employee is upset because he does not know which he should obey, or, (b) different orders may reach him at the same time and he does not know which he should carry out first.

Equally as bad as having two bosses is the situation where the supervisor is by-passed. Let us suppose you are a supervisor whose boss by-passes you (deals directly with people reporting to you). To the worker, it is the same as having two bosses; but to you, the supervisor, it is equally serious. By-passing on the part of your boss will undermine your authority, and the people under you will begin looking to your boss for decisions and even for routine orders.

You can prevent by-passing by telling the people you supervise that if anyone tries to give them orders, they should direct that person to you.

Span of Control

Span of control on a given level involves:

   a. The number of people being supervised
   b. The distance
   c. The time involved in supervising the people. (One supervisor cannot supervise too many workers effectively.)

Span of control means that a supervisor has the right number (not too many and not too few) of subordinates that he can supervise well.

<u>Uniformity of Assignment</u>

In assigning work, you as the supervisor should assign to each person jobs that are similar in nature. An employee who is assigned too many different types of jobs will waste time in going from one kind of work to another. It takes time for him to get to top production in one kind of task and, before he does so, he has to start on another.

When you assign work to people, remember that:

a. Job duties should be definite. Make it clear from the beginning <u>what</u> they are to do, <u>how</u> they are to do it, and <u>why</u> they are to do it. Let them know how much they are expected to do and how well they are expected to do it.

b. Check your assignments to be certain that there are no workers with too many unrelated duties, and that no two people have been given overlapping responsibilities. Your aim should be to have every task assigned to a specific person with the work fairly distributed and with each person doing his part.

<u>Assignment of Responsibility and Delegation of Authority</u>

A supervisor cannot delegate his final responsibility for the work of his department. The experienced supervisor knows that he gets his work done through people. He can't do it all himself. So he must assign the work and the responsibility for the work to his employees. Then they must be given the authority to carry out their responsibilities.

By assigning responsibility and delegating authority to carry out the responsibility, the supervisor builds in his workers initiative, resourcefulness, enthusiasm, and interest in their work. He is treating them as responsible adults. They can find satisfaction in their work, and they will respect the supervisor and be loyal to the supervisor.

PRINCIPLES OF ORGANIZATION

1. <u>Definition</u>
   Organization is the method of dividing up the work to provide the best channels for coordinated effort to get the agency's mission accomplished.

2. <u>Purpose of Organization</u>
   a. To enable each employee within the organization to clearly know his responsibilities and relationships to his fellow employees and to organizational units.
   b. To avoid conflicts of authority and overlapping of jurisdiction.
   c. To ensure teamwork.

3. Basic Considerations in Organizational Planning
   a. The basic plans and objectives of the agency should be deter-
      mined, and the organizational structure should be adapted to
      carry out effectively such plans and objectives.
   b. The organization should be built around the major functions
      of the agency and not individuals or groups of individuals.
   c. The organization should be sufficiently flexible to meet new
      and changing conditions which may be brought about from
      within or outside the department.
   d. The organizational structure should be as simple as possible
      and the number of organizational units kept at a minimum.
   e. The number of levels of authority should be kept at a minimum.
      Each additional management level lengthens the chain of
      authority and responsibility and increases the time for
      instructions to be distributed to operating levels and for
      decisions to be obtained from higher authority.
   f. The form of organization should permit each executive to
      exercise maximum initiative within the limits of delegated
      authority.

4. Bases for Organization
   a. Purpose (Examples: education, police, sanitation)
   b. Process (Examples: accounting, legal, purchasing)
   c. Clientele (Examples: welfare, parks, veteran)
   d. Geographic (Examples: borough offices, precincts, libraries)

5. Assignments of Functions
   a. Every function of the agency should be assigned to a specific
      organizational unit. Under normal circumstances, no single
      function should be assigned to more than one organizational
      unit.
   b. There should be no overlapping, duplication, or conflict
      between organizational elements.
   c. Line functions should be separated from staff functions, and
      proper emphasis should be placed on staff activities.
   d. Functions which are closely related or similar should
      normally be assigned to a single organizational unit.
   e. Functions should be properly distributed to promote balance,
      and to avoid overemphasis of less important functions and
      underemphasis of more essential functions.

6. Delegation of Authority and Responsibility
   a. Responsibilities assigned to a specific individual or organi-
      zational unit should carry corresponding authority, and all
      statements of authority or limitations thereof should be as
      specific as possible.
   b. Authority and responsibility for action should be decentralized
      to organizational units and individuals responsible for actual
      performance to the greatest extent possible, without relaxing
      necessary control over policy or the standardization of pro-
      cedures. Delegation of authority will be consistent with
      decentralization of responsibility but such delegation will
      not divest an executive in higher authority of his overall
      responsibility.

c. The heads of organizational units should concern themselves
with important matters and should delegate to the maximum
extent details and routines performed in the ordinary course
of business.
d. All responsibilities, authorities, and relationships should
be stated in simple language to avoid misinterpretation.
e. Each individual or organizational unit charged with a
specific responsibility will be held responsible for results.

7. Employee Relationships
a. The employees reporting to one executive should not exceed
the number which can be effectively directed and coordinated.
The number will depend largely upon the scope and extent of
the responsibilities of the subordinates.
b. No person should report to more than one supervisor. Every
supervisor should know who reports to him, and every employee
should know to whom he reports. Channels of authority and
responsibility should not be violated by staff units.
c. Relationships between organizational units within the agency
and with outside organizations and associations should be
clearly stated and thoroughly understood to avoid misunder-
standing.

DELEGATING

1. What is Delegating?
Delegating is assigning a job to an employee, giving him the
authority to get that job done, and giving him the responsibility
for seeing to it that the job is done.

a. What to Delegate
(1) Routine details
(2) Jobs which may be necessary and take a lot of time, but
do not have to be done by the supervisor personally
(preparing reports, attending meetings, etc.)
(3) Routine decision-making (making decisions which do not
require the supervisor's personal attention)

b. What Not to Delegate
(1) Job details which are *executive functions* (setting goals,
organizing employees into a good team, analyzing results
so as to plan for the future)
(2) Disciplinary power (handling grievances, preparing service
ratings, reprimands, etc.)
(3) Decision-making which involves large numbers of employees
or other bureaus and departments
(4) Final and complete responsibility for the job done by the
unit being supervised

c. Why Delegate?
(1) To strengthen the organization by developing a greater
number of skilled employees

(2) To improve the employee's performance by giving him the chance to learn more about the job, handle some responsibility, and become more interested in getting the job done

(3) To improve a supervisor's performance by relieving him of routine jobs and giving him more time for *executive functions* (planning, organizing, controlling, etc.) which cannot be delegated

2. <u>To Whom to Delegate</u>
People with abilities not being used. Selection should be based on ability, not on favoritism.

REPORTS

Definition
A report is an orderly presentation of factual information directed to a specific reader for a specific purpose.

Purpose
The general purpose of a report is to bring to the reader useful and factual information about a condition or a problem. Some specific purposes of a report may be:

1. To enable the reader to appraise the efficiency or effectiveness of a person or an operation
2. To provide a basis for establishing standards
3. To reflect the results of expenditures of time, effort, and money
4. To provide a basis for developing or altering programs

Types

1. Information Report - Contains facts arranged in sequence
2. Summary (Examination) Report - Contains facts plus an analysis or discussion of the significance of the facts. Analysis may give advantages and disadvantages or give qualitative and quantitative comparisons
3. Recommendation Report - Contains facts, analysis, and conclusion logically drawn from the facts and analysis, plus a recommendation based upon the facts, analysis, and conclusions

Factors to Consider Before Writing Report

1. <u>Why</u> write the report - The purpose of the report should be clearly defined.
2. <u>Who</u> will read the report - What level of language should be used? Will the reader understand professional or technical language?
3. <u>What</u> should be said - What does the reader need or want to know about the subject?
4. <u>How</u> should it be said - Should the subject be presented tactfully? Convincingly? In a stimulating manner?

Preparatory Steps

   1. Assemble the facts - Find out who, why, what, where, when, and
      how.
   2. Organize the facts - Eliminate unnecessary information.
   3. Prepare an outline - Check for orderliness, logical sequence.
   4. Prepare a draft - Check for correctness, clearness, complete-
      ness, conciseness, and tone.
   5. Prepare it in final form - Check for grammar, punctuation,
      appearance.

Outline For a Recommendation Report
   Is the report:

   1. Correct in information, grammar, and tone?
   2. Clear?
   3. Complete?
   4. Concise?
   5. Timely?
   6. Worth its cost?

   Will the report accomplish its purpose?

                         MANAGEMENT CONTROLS

1. Control
    What is control? What is controlled? Who controls?

    The essence of control is action which adjusts operations to
    predetermined standards, and its basis is information in the hands
    of managers. Control is checking to determine whether plans are
    being observed and suitable progress toward stated objectives is
    being made, and action is taken, if necessary, to correct devia-
    tions.

    We have a ready-made model for this concept of control in the
    automatic systems which are widely used for process control in
    the chemical and petroleum industries. A process control system
    works this way. Suppose, for example, it is desired to maintain
    a constant rate of flow of oil through a pipe at a predetermined
    or set-point value. A signal, whose strength represents the
    rate of flow, can be produced in a measuring device and trans-
    mitted to a control mechanism. The control mechanism, when it
    detects any deviation of the actual from the set-point signal,
    will reposition the value regulating flow rate.

2. Basis For Control
    A process control mechanism thus acts to adjust operations to
    predetermined standards and does so on the basis of information
    it receives. In a parallel way, information reaching a manager
    gives him the opportunity for corrective action and is his basis
    for control. He cannot exercise control without such informa-
    tion, and he cannot do a complete job of managing without
    controlling.

3. <u>Policy</u>
   <u>What is policy?</u>

   Policy is simply a statement of an organization's intention to act in certain ways when specified types of circumstances arise. It represents a general decision, predetermined and expressed as a principle or rule, establishing a normal pattern of conduct for dealing with given types of business events - usually recurrent. A statement is therefore useful in economizing the time of managers and in assisting them to discharge their responsibilities equitably and consistently.

   Policy is not a means of control, but policy does generate the need for control.

   Adherence to policies is not guaranteed nor can it be taken on faith. It has to be verified. Without verification, there is no basis for control. Policy and procedures, although closely related and interdependent to a certain extent, are not synonymous. A policy may be adopted, for example, to maintain a materials inventory not to exceed one million dollars. A procedure for inventory control would interpret that policy and convert it into methods for keeping within that limit, with consideration, too, of possible but foreseeable expedient deviation.

4. <u>Procedure</u>
   <u>What is procedure?</u>

   A procedure specifically prescribes:

   a. What work is to be performed by the various participants
   b. Who are the respective participants
   c. When and where the various steps in the different processes are to be performed
   d. The sequence of operations that will insure uniform handling of recurring transactions
   e. The *paper* that is involved, its origin, transition, and disposition

   Necessary appurtenances to a procedure are:

   a. Detailed organizational chart
   b. Flow charts
   c. Exhibits of forms, all presented in close proximity to the text of the procedure

5. <u>Basis of Control - Information in the Hands of Managers</u>
   <u>If the basis of control is information in the hands of managers,</u> then <u>reporting</u> is elevated to a level of very considerable importance.

Types of reporting may include:

    a. Special reports and routine reports
    b. Written, oral, and graphic reports
    c. Staff meetings
    d. Conferences
    e. Television screens
    f. Non-receipt of information, as where management is by exception
    g. Any other means whereby information is transmitted to a manager as a basis for control action

FRAMEWORK OF MANAGEMENT

Elements

1. Policy - It has to be verified, controlled.

2. Organization - is part of the giving of an assignment. The organizational chart gives to each individual in his title, a first approximation of the nature of his assignment and orients him as being accountable to a certain individual. Organization is not in a true sense a means of control. Control is checking to ascertain whether the assignment is executed as intended and acting on the basis of that information.

3. Budgets - perform three functions:

    a. They present the objectives, plans, and programs of the organization in financial terms.
    b. They report the progress of actual performance against these predetermined objectives, plans, and programs.
    c. Like organizational charts, delegations of authority, procedures and job descriptions, they define the assignments which have flowed from the Chief Executive.

Budgets are a means of control in the respect that they report progress of actual performance against the program. They provide information which enables managers to take action directed toward bringing actual results into conformity with the program.

4. Internal Check - provides in practice for the principle that the same person should not have responsibility for all phases of a transaction. This makes it clearly an aspect of organization rather than of control. Internal Check is static, or built-in.

5. Plans, Programs, Objectives
People must know what they are trying to do. Objectives fulfill this need. Without them, people may work industriously and yet, working aimlessly, accomplish little. Plans and

Programs complement Objectives, since they propose how and according to what time schedule the objectives are to be reached.

6. Delegations of Authority
   Among the ways we have for supplementing the titles and lines of authority of an organizational chart are delegations of authority. Delegations of authority clarify the extent of authority of individuals and in that way serve to define assignments. That they are not means of control is apparent from the very fact that wherever there has been a delegation of authority, the need for control increases. This could hardly be expected to happen if delegations of authority were themselves means of control.

Manager's Responsibility

Control becomes necessary whenever a manager delegates authority to a subordinate because he cannot delegate and then simply sit back and forget all about it. A manager's accountability to his own superior has not diminished one whit as a result of delegating part of his authority to a subordinate. The manager must exercise control over actions taken under the authority so delegated. That means checking serves as a basis for possible corrective action.

Objectives, plans, programs, organizational charts, and other elements of the managerial system are not fruitfully regarded as either controls or means of control. They are pre-established standards or models of performance to which operations are adjusted by the exercise of management control. These standards or models of performance are dynamic in character for they are constantly altered, modified, or revised. Policies, organizational set-up, procedures, delegations, etc. are constantly altered but, like objectives and plans, they remain in force until they are either abandoned or revised. All of the elements (or standards or models of performance), objectives, plans and programs, policies, organization, etc. can be regarded as a *framework of management*.

Control Techniques

Examples of control techniques:

1. Compare against established standards
2. Compare with a similar operation
3. Compare with past operations
4. Compare with predictions of accomplishment

Where Forecasts Fit

Control is after-the-fact while forecasts are before. Forecasts and projections are important for setting objectives and formulating plans.

Information for aiming and planning does not have to before-the-fact. It may be an after-the-fact analysis proving that a certain policy has been impolitic in its effect on the relation of the company or department with customer, employee, taxpayer, or stockholder; or that a certain plan is no longer practical, or that a certain procedure is unworkable.

The prescription here certainly would not be in control (in these cases, control would simply bring operations into conformity with obsolete standards) but the establishment of new standards, a new policy, a new plan, and a new procedure to be controlled too.

Information is, of course, the basis for all communication in addition to furnishing evidence to management of the need for reconstructing the framework of management.

PROBLEM SOLVING

The accepted concept in modern management for problem solving is the utilization of the following steps:

1. Identify the problem
2. Gather data
3. List possible solutions
4. Test possible solutions
5. Select the best solution
6. Put the solution into actual practice

Occasions might arise where you would have to apply the second step of gathering data before completing the first step.

You might also find that it will be necessary to work on several steps at the same time.

1. Identify the Problem

Your first step is to define as precisely as possible the problem to be solved. While this may sound easy, it is often the most difficult part of the process.

It has been said of problem solving that you are halfway to the solution when you can write out a clear statement of the problem itself.

Our job now is to get below the surface manifestations of the trouble and pinpoint the problem. This is usually accomplished by a logical analysis, by going from the general to the particular; from the obvious to the not-so-obvious cause.

Let us say that production is behind schedule. WHY? Absenteeism is high. Now, is absenteeism the basic problem to be tackled, or is it merely a symptom of low morale among the workforce? Under these circumstances, you may decide that production is not the problem; the problem is *employee morale*.

In trying to define the problem, remember there is seldom one simple reason why production is lagging, or reports are late, etc.

Analysis usually leads to the discovery that an apparent problem is really made up of several subproblems which must be attacked separately.

Another way is to limit the problem, and thereby ease the task of finding a solution, and concentrate on the elements which are within the scope of your control.

When you have gone this far, write out a tentative statement of the problem to be solved.

2. Gather Data

In the second step, you must set out to collect all the information that might have a bearing on the problem. Do not settle for an assumption when reasonable fact and figures are available.

If you merely go through the motions of problem-solving, you will probably shortcut the information-gathering step. Therefore, do not stack the evidence by confining your research to your own preconceived ideas.

As you collect facts, organize them in some form that helps you make sense of them and   spot possible relationships between them. For example: Plotting cost per unit figures on a graph can be more meaningful than a long column of figures.

Evaluate each item as you go along. Is the source material: absolutely reliable, probably reliable, or not to be trusted.

One of the best methods for gathering data is to go out and look the situation over carefully. Talk to the people on the job who are most affected by this problem.

Always keep in mind that a primary source is usually better than a secondary source of information.

3. List Possible Solutions

This is the creative thinking step of problem solving. This is a good time to bring into play whatever techniques of group dynamics the agency or bureau might have developed for a joint attack on problems.

Now the important thing for you to do is: Keep an open mind. Let your imagination roam freely over the facts you have collected. Jot down every possible solution that occurs to you. Resist the temptation to evaluate various proposals as you go along. List seemingly absurd ideas along with more plausible ones. The more possibilities you list during this step, the less risk you will run of settling for merely a workable, rather than the best, solution.

Keep studying the data as long as there seems to be any chance of deriving additional - ideas, solutions, explanations, or patterns from it.

4. Test Possible Solutions

Now you begin to evaluate the possible solutions. Take pains to be objective. Up to this point, you have suspended judgment but you might be tempted to select a solution you secretly favored all along and proclaim it as the best of the lot.

The secret of objectivity in this phase is to test the possible solutions separately, measuring each against a common yardstick. To make this yardstick try to enumerate as many specific criteria as you can think of. Criteria are best phrased as questions which you ask of each possible solution. They can be drawn from these general categories:

Suitability - Will this solution do the job?
            Will it solve the problem completely or
              partially?
            Is it a permanent or a stopgap solution?

Feasibility - Will this plan work in actual practice?
            Can we afford this approach?
            How much will it cost?

Acceptability - Will the boss go along with the changes
              required in the plan?
            Are we trying to drive a tack with a sledge
              hammer?

5. Select the Best Solution

This is the area of executive decision.

Occasionally, one clearly superior solution will stand out at the conclusion of the testing process. But often it is not that simple. You may find that no one solution has come through all the tests with flying colors.

You may also find that a proposal, which flunked miserably on one of the essential tests, racked up a very high score on others.

The best solution frequently will turn out to be a combination.

Try to arrange a marriage that will bring together the strong points of one possible solution with the particular virtues of another. The more skill and imagination that you apply, the greater is the likelihood that you will come out with a solution that is not merely adequate and workable, but is the best possible under the circumstances.

6. <u>Put the Solution Into Actual Practice</u>

As every executive knows, a plan which works perfectly on paper may develop all sorts of bugs when put into actual practice.

Problem-solving does not stop with selecting the solution which looks best in theory.

The next step is to put the chosen solution into action and watch the results. The results may point towards modifications.

If the problem disappears when you put your solution into effect, you know you have the right solution.

If it does not disappear, even after you have adjusted your plan to cover unforeseen difficulties that turned up in practice, work your way back through the problem-solving solutions.

    Would one of them have worked better?
    Did you overlook some vital piece of data which would have
        given you a different slant on the whole situation?
    Did you apply all necessary criteria in testing solutions?
    If no light dawns after this much rechecking, it is a pretty
        good bet that you defined the problem incorrectly in the
        first place.

You came up with the wrong solution because you tackled the wrong problem.

Thus, step six may become step one of a new problem-solving cycle.

COMMUNICATION

1. <u>What is Communication?</u>
We communicate through writing, speaking, action or inaction. In speaking to people face-to-face, there is opportunity to judge reactions and to adjust the message. This makes the supervisory chain one of the most, and in many instances the most, important channels of communication.

In an organization, communication means keeping employees informed about the organization's objectives, policies, problems, and progress. Communication is the free interchange of information, ideas, and desirable attitudes between and among employees and between employees and management.

2. <u>Why is Communication Needed?</u>
   a. People have certain social needs
   b. Good communication is essential in meeting those social needs
   c. While people have similar basic needs, at the same time they
      differ from each other
   d. Communication must be adapted to these individual differences

An employee cannot do his best work unless he knows why he is doing it. If he has the feeling that he is being kept in the dark about what is going on, his enthusiasm and productivity suffer.

Effective communication is needed in an organization so that employees will understand what the organization is trying to accomplish; and how the work of one unit contributes to or affects the work of other units in the organization and other organizations.

3. How is Communication Achieved?
   Communication flows downward, upward, sideways.

   a. Communication may come from top management down to employees. This is downward communication.

      Some means of downward communication are:
      (1) Training (orientation, job instruction, supervision, public relations, etc.)
      (2) Conferences
      (3) Staff meetings
      (4) Policy statements
      (5) Bulletins
      (6) Newsletters
      (7) Memoranda
      (8) Circulation of important letters

      In downward communication, it is important that employees be informed in advance of changes that will affect them.

   b. Communications should also be developed so that the ideas, suggestions, and knowledge of employees will flow upward to top management.

      Some means of upward communication are:
      (1) Personal discussion conferences
      (2) Committees
      (3) Memoranda
      (4) Employees suggestion program
      (5) Questionnaires to be filled in giving comments and suggestions about proposed actions that will affect field operations

      Upward communication requires that management be willing to listen, to accept, and to make changes when good ideas are present. Upward communication succeeds when there is no fear of punishment for speaking out or lack of interest at the top. Employees will share their knowledge and ideas with management when interest is shown and recognition is given.

   c. The *advantages* of downward communication:
     (1) It enables the passing down of orders, policies, and plans necessary to the continued operation of the station.
     (2) By making information available, it diminishes the fears and suspicions which result from misinformation and misunderstanding.
     (3) It fosters the pride people want to have in their work when they are told of good work.
     (4) It improves the morale and stature of the individual to be *in the know*.
     (5) It helps employees to understand, accept, and cooperate with changes when they know about them in advance.

   d. The *advantages* of upward communication:
     (1) It enables the passing upward of information, attitudes, and feelings.
     (2) It makes it easier to find out how ready people are to receive downward communication.
     (3) It reveals the degree to which the downward communication is understood and accepted.
     (4) It helps to satisfy the basic *social* needs.
     (5) It stimulates employees to participate in the operation of their organization.
     (6) It encourages employees to contribute ideas for improving the efficiency and economy of operations.
     (7) It helps to solve problem situations before they reach the explosion point.

4. **Why Does Communication Fail?**
   a. The technical difficulties of conveying information clearly
   b. The emotional content of communication which prevents complete transmission
   c. The fact that there is a difference between what management needs to say, what it wants to say, and what it does say
   d. The fact that there is a difference between what employees would like to say, what they think is profitable or safe to say, and what they do say

5. **How to Improve Communication.**
As a supervisor, you are a key figure in communication. To improve as a communicator, you should:
   a. Know - Knowing your subordinates will help you to recognize and work with individual differences.
   b. Like - If you like those who work for you and those for whom you work, this will foster the kind of friendly, warm, work atmosphere that will facilitate communication.
   c. Trust - Showing a sincere desire to communicate will help to develop the mutual trust and confidence which are essential to the free flow of communication.

    d. <u>Tell</u> - Tell your subordinates and superiors *what's doing*.
       <u>Tell</u> your subordinates *why* as well as *how*.
    e. <u>Listen</u> - By listening, you help others to talk and you
       create good listeners. Don't forget that listening implies
       action.
    f. <u>Stimulate</u> - Communication has to be stimulated and encouraged.
       Be receptive to ideas and suggestions and motivate your
       people so that each member of the team identifies himself
       with the job at hand.
    g. <u>Consult</u> - The most effective way of consulting is to let your
       people participate, insofar as possible, in developing
       determinations which affect them or their work.

6. <u>How to Determine Whether You are Getting Across.</u>
    a. Check to see that communication is received and understood
    b. Judge this understanding by actions rather than words
    c. Adapt or vary communication, when necessary
    d. Remember that good communication cannot cure all problems

7. <u>The Key Attitude.</u>
Try to see things from the other person's point of view. By
doing this, you help to develop the permissive atmosphere and
the shared confidence and understanding which are essential to
effective two-way communication.

Communication is a two-way process.
    a. The basic purpose of any communication is to get action.
    b. The only way to get action is through **acceptance**.
    c. In order to get acceptance, communication must be humanly
       satisfying as well as technically efficient.

HOW ORDERS AND INSTRUCTIONS SHOULD BE GIVEN

<u>Characteristics of Good Orders and Instructions</u>

1. <u>Clear</u>
Orders should be definite as to
  - <u>What</u> is to be done
  - <u>Who</u> is to do it
  - <u>When</u> it is to be done
  - <u>Where</u> it is to be done
  - <u>How</u> it is to be done

2. <u>Concise</u>
Avoid wordiness. Orders should be brief and to the point.

3. <u>Timely</u>
Instructions and orders should be sent out at the proper time
and not too long in advance of expected performance.

4. <u>Possibility of Performance</u>
   Orders should be feasible:
   a. Investigate before giving orders
   b. Consult those who are to carry out instructions before
      formulating and issuing them

5. <u>Properly Directed</u>
   Give the orders to the people concerned. Do not send orders to
   people who are not concerned. People who continually receive
   instructions that are not applicable to them get in the habit
   of neglecting instructions generally.

6. <u>Reviewed Before Issuance</u>
   Orders should be reviewed before issuance:
   a. Test them by putting yourself in the position of the recipient
   b. If they involve new procedures, have the persons who are to do
      the work review them for suggestions

7. <u>Reviewed After Issuance</u>
   Persons who receive orders should be allowed to raise questions
   and to point out unforeseen consequences of orders.

8. <u>Coordinated</u>
   Orders should be coordinated so that work runs smoothly.

9. <u>Courteous</u>
   Make a request rather than a demand. There is no need to
   continually call attention to the fact that you are the boss.

10. <u>Recognizable as an Order</u>
    Be sure that the order is recognizable as such.

11. <u>Complete</u>
    Be sure recipient has knowledge and experience sufficient to
    carry out order. Give illustrations and examples.

A DEPARTMENTAL PERSONNEL OFFICE IS RESPONSIBLE FOR THE FOLLOWING FUNCTIONS

1. Policy
2. Personnel Programs
3. Recruitment and Placement
4. Position Classification
5. Salary and Wage Administration
6. Employee Performance Standards and Evaluation
7. Employee Relations
8. Disciplinary Actions and Separations
9. Health and Safety
10. Staff Training and Development
11. Personnel Records, Procedures, and Reports
12. Employee Services
13. Personnel Research

SUPERVISION

Leadership

All leadership is based essentially on authority. This comes from two sources: it is received from higher management or it is earned by the supervisor through his methods of supervision. Although effective leadership has always depended upon the leader's using his authority in such a way as to appeal successfully to the motives of the people supervised, the conditions for making this appeal are continually changing. The key to today's problem of leadership is flexibility and resourcefulness on the part of the leader in meeting changes in conditions as they occur.

Three basic approaches to leadership are generally recognized:

1. The Authoritarian Approach
   a. The methods and techniques used in this approach emphasize the *I* in leadership and depend primarily on the formal authority of the leader. This authority is sometimes exercised in a hardboiled manner and sometimes in a benevolent manner, but in either case the dominating role of the leader is reflected in the thinking, planning, and decisions of the group.
   b. Group results are to a large degree dependent on close supervision by the leader. Usually, the individuals in the group will not show a high degree of initiative or acceptance of responsibility and their capacity to grow and develop probably will not be fully utilized. The group may react with resentment or submission, depending upon the manner and skill of the leader in using his authority
   c. This approach develops as a natural outgrowth of the authority that goes with the leader's job and his feeling of sole responsibility for getting the job done. It is relatively easy to use and does not require much resourcefulness.
   d. The use of this approach is effective in times of emergencies, in meeting close deadlines as a final resort, in settling some issues, in disciplinary matters, and with dependent individuals and groups.

2. The Laissez-Faire or *Let 'em Alone* Approach
   a. This approach generally is characterized by an avoidance of leadership responsibility by the leader. The activities of the group depend largely on the choice of its members rather than the leader.
   b. Group results probably will be poor. Generally, there will be disagreements over petty things, bickering, and confusion. Except for a few aggressive people, individuals will not show much initiative and growth and development will be retarded. There may be a tendency for informal leaders to take over leadership of the group.
   c. This approach frequently results from the leader's dislike of responsibility, from his lack of confidence, from failure of other methods to work, from disappointment or criticism.

It is usually the easiest of the three to use and requires both understanding and resourcefulness on the part of the leader.

d. This approach is occasionally useful and effective, particularly in forcing dependent individuals or groups to rely on themselves, to give someone a chance to save face by clearing his own difficulties, or when action should be delayed temporarily for good cause.

3. The Democratic Approach

a. The methods and techniques used in this approach emphasize the *we* in leadership and build up the responsibility of the group to attain its objectives. Reliance is placed largely on the earned authority of the leader.

b. Group results are likely to be good because most of the job motives of the people will be satisfied. Cooperation and teamwork, initiative, acceptance of responsibility, and the individual's capacity for growth probably will show a high degree of development.

c. This approach grows out of a desire or necessity of the leader to find ways to appeal effectively to the motivation of his group. It is the best approach to build up inside the person a strong desire to cooperate and apply himself to the job. It is the most difficult to develop, and requires both understanding and resourcefulness on the part of the leader.

d. The value of this approach increases over a long period where sustained efficiency and development of people are important. It may not be fully effective in all situations, however, particularly when there is not sufficient time to use it properly or where quick decisions must be made.

All three approaches are used by most leaders and have a place in supervising people. The extent of their use varies with individual leaders, with some using one approach predominantly. The leader who uses these three approaches, and varies their use with time and circumstance, is probably the most effective. Leadership which is used predominantly with a democratic approach requires more resourcefulness on the part of the leader but offers the greatest possibilities in terms of teamwork and cooperation.

The one best way of developing democratic leadership is to provide a real sense of participation on the part of the group, since this satisfies most of the chief job motives. Although there are many ways of providing participation, consulting as frequently as possible with individuals and groups on things that affect them seems to offer the most in building cooperation and responsibility. Consultation takes different forms, but it is most constructive when people feel they are actually helping in finding the answers to the problems on the job.

There are some requirements of leaders in respect to human relations which should be considered in their selection and development. Generally, the leader should be interested in working with other people, emotionally stable, self-confident, and sensitive to the reactions of others. In addition, his viewpoint should be one of getting the job done through people who work cooperatively in response to his leadership. He should have a knowledge of individual and group behavior, but, most important of all, he should work to combine all of these requirements into a definite, practical skill in leadership.

Nine Points of Contrast Between *Boss* and *Leader*

1. The boss drives his men; the leader coaches them.
2. The boss depends on authority; the leader on good will.
3. The boss inspires fear; the leader inspires enthusiasm.
4. The boss says *I*; the leader says *We*.
5. The boss says *Get here on time*; the leader gets there ahead of time.
6. The boss fixes the blame for the breakdown; the leader fixes the breakdown.
7. The boss knows how it is done; the leader shows how.
8. The boss makes work a drudgery; the leader makes work a game.
9. The boss says *Go*; the leader says *Let's go*.

EMPLOYEE MORALE

Employee morale is the way employees feel about each other, the organization or unit in which they work, and the work they perform.

Some Ways to Develop and Maintain Good Employee Morale

1. Give adequate credit and praise when due.
2. Recognize importance of all jobs and equalize load with proper assignments, always giving consideration to personality differences and abilities.
3. Welcome suggestions and do not have an *all-wise* attitude. Request employees' assistance in solving problems and use assistants when conducting group meetings on certain subjects.
4. Properly assign responsibilities and give adequate authority for fulfillment of such assignments.
5. Keep employees informed about matters that affect them.
6. Criticize and reprimand employees privately.
7. Be accessible and willing to listen.
8. Be fair.
9. Be alert to detect training possibilities so that you will not miss an opportunity to help each employee do a better job, and if possible with less effort on his part.
10. Set a good example.
11. Apply the golden rule.

Some Indicators of Good Morale

1. Good quality of work
2. Good quantity
3. Good attitude of employees

4. Good discipline
5. Teamwork
6. Good attendance
7. Employee participation

MOTIVATION

Drives

A *drive*, stated simply, is a desire or force which causes a person to do or say certain things. These are some of the most usual drives and some of their identifying characteristics recognizable in people motivated by such drives:

1. Security (desire to provide for the future)
   Always on time for work
   Works for the same employer for many years
   Never takes unnecessary chances
   Seldom resists doing what he is told

2. Recognition (desire to be rewarded for accomplishment)
   Likes to be asked for his opinion
   Becomes very disturbed when he makes a mistake
   Does things to attract attention
   Likes to see his name in print

3. Position (desire to hold certain status in relation to others)
   Boasts about important people he knows
   Wants to be known as a key man
   Likes titles
   Demands respect
   Belongs to clubs, for prestige

4. Accomplishment (desire to get things done)
   Complains when things are held up
   Likes to do things that have tangible results
   Never lies down on the job
   Is proud of turning out good work

5. Companionship (desire to associate with other people)
   Likes to work with others
   Tells stories and jokes
   Indulges in horseplay
   Finds excuses to talk to others on the job

6. Possession (desire to collect and hoard objects)
   Likes to collect things
   Puts his name on things belonging to him
   Insists on the same work location

Supervisors may find that identifying the drives of employees is a helpful step toward motivating them to self-improvement and better job performance. For example: An employee's job performance is below average. His supervisor, having previously determined that the employee is motivated by a drive for security, suggests that taking training courses will help the employee to improve, advance, and earn more money. Since earning more money can be a step toward greater security, the employee's drive for security would motivate him to take the training suggested by the supervisor. In essence, this is the process of charting an employee's future course by using his motivating drives to positive advantage.

EMPLOYEE PARTICIPATION

What is Participation?

Employee participation is the employee's giving freely of his time, skill and knowledge to an extent which cannot be obtained by demand.

Why is it Important?

The supervisor's responsibility is to get the job done through people. A good supervisor gets the job done through people who work willingly and well. The participation of employees is important because:

1. Employees develop a greater sense of responsibility when they share in working out operating plans and goals.
2. Participation provides greater opportunity and stimulation for employees to learn, and to develop their ability.
3. Participation sometimes provides better solutions to problems because such solutions may combine the experience and knowledge of interested employees who want the solutions to work.
4. An employee or group may offer a solution which the supervisor might hesitate to make for fear of demanding too much.
5. Since the group wants to make the solution work, they exert *pressure* in a constructive way on each other.
6. Participation usually results in reducing the need for close supervision.

How May Supervisors Obtain It?

Participation is encouraged when employees feel that they share some responsibility for the work and that their ideas are sincerely wanted and valued. Some ways of obtaining employee participation are:

1. Conduct orientation programs for new employees to inform them about the organization and their rights and responsibilities as employees.

2. Explain the aims and objectives of the agency. On a continuing basis, be sure that the employees know what these aims and objectives are.
3. Share job successes and responsibilities and give credit for success.
4. Consult with employees, both as individuals and in groups, about things that affect them.
5. Encourage suggestions for job improvements. Help employees to develop good suggestions. The suggestions can bring them recognition. The city's suggestion program offers additional encouragement through cash awards.

The supervisor who encourages employee participation is not surrendering his authority. He must still make decisions and initiate action, and he must continue to be ultimately responsible for the work of those he supervises. But, through employee participation, he is helping his group to develop greater ability and a sense of responsibility while getting the job done faster and better.

STEPS IN HANDLING A GRIEVANCE

1. Get the facts
   a. Listen sympathetically.
   b. Let him talk himself out.
   c. Get his story straight.
   d. Get his point of view.
   e. Don't argue with him.
   f. Give him plenty of time.
   g. Conduct the interview privately.
   h. Don't try to shift the blame or pass the buck.

2. Consider the facts
   a. Consider the employee's viewpoint.
   b. How will the decision affect similar cases.
   c. Consider each decision as a possible precedent.
   d. Avoid snap judgments - don't jump to conclusions.

3. Make or get a decision
   a. Frame an effective counter-proposal.
   b. Make sure it is fair to all.
   c. Have confidence in your judgment.
   d. Be sure you can substantiate your decision.

4. Notify the employee of your decision
   Be sure he is told; try to convince him that the decision is fair and just.

5. Take action when needed and if within your authority
   Otherwise, tell employee that the matter will be called to the attention of the proper person or that nothing can be done, and why it cannot.

6. Follow through to see that the desired result is achieved.

7. Record key facts concerning the complaint and the action taken.

8. Leave the way open to him to appeal your decision to a higher authority.

9. Report all grievances to your superior, whether they are appealed or not.

DISCIPLINE

Discipline is training that develops self-control, orderly conduct, and efficiency.

To discipline does not necessarily mean to punish.

To discipline does mean to train, to regulate, and to govern conduct.

The Disciplinary Interview

Most employees sincerely want to do what is expected of them. In other words, they are self-disciplined. Some employees, however, fail to observe established rules and standards, and disciplinary action by the supervisor is required.

The primary purpose of disciplinary action is to improve conduct without creating dissatisfaction, bitterness, or resentment in the process.

Constructive disciplinary action is more concerned with causes and explanations of breaches of conduct than with punishment. The disciplinary interview is held to get at the causes of apparent misbehavior and to motivate better performance in the future.

It is important that the interview be kept on as impersonal a basis as possible. If the supervisor lets the interview descend to the plane of an argument, it loses its effectiveness.

Planning the Interview

Get all pertinent facts concerning the situation so that you can talk in specific terms to the employee.

Review the employee's record, appraisal ratings, etc.

Consider what you know about the temperament of the employee. Consider your attitude toward the employee. Remember that the primary requisite of disciplinary action is fairness.

Don't enter upon the interview when angry.

Schedule the interview for a place which is private and out of hearing of others.

Conducting the Interview

1. Make an effort to establish accord.

2. Question the employee about the apparent breach of discipline. Be sure that the question is not so worded as to be itself an accusation.

3. Give the employee a chance to tell his side of the story. Give him ample opportunity to talk.

4. Use understanding-listening except where it is necessary to ask a question or to point out some details of which the employee may not be aware. If the employee misrepresents facts, make a plain, accurate statement of the facts, but don't argue and don't engage in personal controversy.

5. Listen and try to understand the reasons for the employee's (mis)conduct. First of all, don't assume that there has been a breach of discipline. Evaluate the employee's reasons for his conduct in the light of his opinions and feelings concerning the consistency and reasonableness of the standards which he was expected to follow. Has the supervisor done his part in explaining the reasons for the rules? Was the employee's behavior unintentional or deliberate? Does he think he had real reasons for his actions? What new facts is he telling? Do the facts justify his actions? What causes, other than those mentioned, could have stimulated the behavior?

6. After listening to the employee's version of the situation, and if censure of his actions is warranted, the supervisor should proceed with whatever criticism is justified. Emphasis should be placed on future improvement rather than exclusively on the employee's failure to measure up to expected standards of job conduct.

7. Fit the criticism to the individual. With one employee, a word of correction may be all that is required.

8. Attempt to distinguish between unintentional error and deliberate misbehavior. An error due to ignorance requires training and not censure.

9. Administer criticism in a controlled, even tone of voice, never in anger. Make it clear that you are acting as an agent of the department. In general, criticism should refer to the job or the employee's actions and not to the person. Criticism of the employee's work is not an attack on the individual.

10. Be sure the interview does not destroy the employee's self-confidence. Mention his good qualities and assure him that you feel confident that he can improve his performance.

11. Wherever possible, before the employee leaves the interview, satisfy him that the incident is closed, that nothing more will be said on the subject unless the offense is repeated.

ANSWER SHEET

TEST NO. _____ PART ____ TITLE OF POSITION _____

PLACE OF EXAMINATION _____ DATE ____

(CITY OR TOWN)   (STATE)

RATING

USE THE SPECIAL PENCIL.   MAKE GLOSSY BLACK MARKS.

Questions 1–25, 26–50, 51–75, 76–100, 101–125 each with answer columns A B C D E

Make only ONE mark for each answer.   Additional and stray marks may be
counted as mistakes.   In making corrections, erase errors COMPLETELY.

ANSWER SHEET

USE THE SPECIAL PENCIL.   MAKE GLOSSY BLACK MARKS.

	A	B	C	D	E		A	B	C	D	E		A	B	C	D	E		A	B	C	D	E		A	B	C	D	E
1						26						51						76						101					
2						27						52						77						102					
3						28						53						78						103					
4						29						54						79						104					
5						30						55						80						105					
6						31						56						81						106					
7						32						57						82						107					
8						33						58						83						108					
9						34						59						84						109					
10						35						60						85						110					

Make only ONE mark for each answer.   Additional and stray marks may be
counted as mistakes.   In making corrections, erase errors COMPLETELY.

	A	B	C	D	E		A	B	C	D	E		A	B	C	D	E		A	B	C	D	E		A	B	C	D	E
11						36						61						86						111					
12						37						62						87						112					
13						38						63						88						113					
14						39						64						89						114					
15						40						65						90						115					
16						41						66						91						116					
17						42						67						92						117					
18						43						68						93						118					
19						44						69						94						119					
20						45						70						95						120					
21						46						71						96						121					
22						47						72						97						122					
23						48						73						98						123					
24						49						74						99						124					
25						50						75						100						125					